AI
Unveiled

A Comprehensive Exploration
from Origins to Modern Developments

Daniel Martinez

Table of Contents

Introduction

Artificial intelligence (AI) is at the vanguard and the cornerstone of the current technological renaissance, bringing breakthroughs that were previously limited to science fiction to life and radically changing our world. As we approach the dawn of a new era, it is our responsibility to create a thorough knowledge of this revolutionary occurrence. The comprehensive e-book " AI Unveiled: A Comprehensive Exploration from Origins to Modern Developments" will help you navigate the dynamic present of AI, put together its complex past, and foresee its bright future.

This e-book takes the reader on a philosophical journey to investigate the ideas that laid the groundwork for artificial intelligence. This historical journey will take us from the philosophies of prehistoric societies to Alan Turing's monumental discoveries in the 20th century, tracing the origins and development of artificial intelligence. Our adventure takes us through a vibrant environment where self-learning machines, neural networks, and autonomous entities coexist, where creativity and imagination are unrestricted.

This all-inclusive book, which is meant to serve both beginners and specialists, explains the fundamental ideas that underpin artificial intelligence (AI) in a way that is both understandable and compelling. It is enhanced with colorful examples and practical applications. We explore the wide range of fields in which artificial intelligence has left a lasting impact, from the revolutions in healthcare to the profound changes in the finance and automobile industries. We will also negotiate the complex web of contemporary tools and technology that underpin AI's relentless advancement alongside.

As we go, we come upon the ethical challenges and difficulties that come with AI's breakthroughs. In an increasingly automated world that can simulate human intelligence, security, equity, and privacy are being put to the test. This e-book aims to stimulate a critical conversation about these urgent problems by getting readers to think about the larger effects of a society where artificial intelligence is widespread.

We investigate the intriguing interaction between artificial intelligence (AI) and popular culture, looking beyond the boundaries of technology and ethics to examine the mutually beneficial relationship that shapes society's expectations and views of AI. Additionally, our goal is to provide you with useful knowledge and advice so you can interact with AI in a proactive manner and create a positive, harmonious relationship with this game-changing technology.

Join us as we explore the rapidly growing field of artificial intelligence, learning about its historical roots, contemporary advancements, and potential future applications. Together, we will pave the way for understanding and equip ourselves to prosper in an era where innovation and possibility are expected to be redefined by artificial intelligence. Now let's get exploring!

CHAPTER I

Origins and History
of Artificial Intelligence

The philosophical foundations: Can machines think?

As the realm of artificial intelligence (AI) expands, one question reverberates at its core, echoing the contemplations of many great minds through centuries: "Can machines think?" This seemingly straightforward question opens the gateway to a labyrinth of philosophical investigations that seek to delineate the nuances of consciousness, intelligence, and the potentialities of machine cognition. It encourages us to venture into metaphysics, epistemology, and ethics, inviting a dialogue that bridges technology, philosophy, modernity, and antiquity.

Since time immemorial, humans have been fascinated with replicating their likeness in machines, a vision that has been vividly painted in folklore, myth, and literature. Early Greek myths recounted tales of artificial beings like Pygmalion's sculpture, transcending the boundaries between the inert and the sentient. But it was not until the advent of the computing era that these myths began to flirt with reality, heralding the dawn of an epoch where machines with cognitive abilities could become more than just figments of human imagination. This shift in perspective marked the embryonic stages of a journey to unravel the philosophical underpinnings of artificial intelligence.

At the epicenter of this discourse stands the figure of Alan Turing, a mathematician and logician who bestowed upon the world a seminal hypothesis that sought to empirically explore machine cognition. In 1950, Turing presented a simple yet profound query: Can machines think? Turing proposed a behavioral approach to address this question, devising a test where an ability of a machine to show intelligent behavior equivalent to or indistinguishable from a human's would serve as the benchmark. As it came to be known, this Turing Test proposed that if a machine could engage in a conversation with a human evaluator such that the evaluator could not reliably tell the machine from the human, the machine is said to be thinking.

Yet, the Turing Test opened a Pandora's box of philosophical inquiries. It urged philosophers and scientists alike to question the nature of consciousness, a realm previously untouched by empirical scrutiny. It beckoned us to dissect the layers of cognitive faculties that govern human intelligence and whether these could be replicated artificially. This led to explorations into the realms of symbolic AI, where machines were programmed to mimic human-like reasoning through the manipulation of symbols, and connectionism, which posited that cognitive processes could be understood as neural networks, complex interconnected webs of simpler units.

Amid these technical examinations, a philosophical problem persisted: could the replication of cognitive processes in a machine grant it consciousness, or would it remain an automaton, devoid of awareness and understanding? This beckoned a deeper exploration into the essence of 'thinking.' Philosophers like John Searle countered the Turing Test's implications with thought experiments like the Chinese Room, arguing that syntactic manipulation of symbols exhibited by computers could not give rise to semantic understanding, an intrinsic characteristic of human cognition. According to Searle, a machine could simulate understanding without genuinely 'understanding' in the human sense, thereby not truly 'thinking.'

Contrarily, proponents of 'Strong AI' maintained that machines could potentially embody mind and consciousness, not just replicate them. This school of thought, buoyed by developments in neural networks and deep learning, embraced the possibility of machines evolving to become entities with cognitive faculties akin to humans, transcending mere symbolic processing to encompass semantic understanding and learning from experiences. This belief engenders a vision where machines are not just tools, but collaborators, learning and evolving with humans in a symbiotic relationship.

Furthermore, the discourse extends into ethical dimensions, bringing forth questions about the rights and responsibilities of sentient machines. If machines were to attain a level of cognition comparable to humans, what ethical considerations would govern their existence? This encourages reevaluating concepts such as consciousness, personhood, and morality, necessitating a paradigm shift in our understanding of these notions. Moreover, it contemplates the potential for machine autonomy, fostering debates on the implications of creating beings capable of independent thought and action.

As artificial intelligence continues to permeate various facets of human life, the question, "Can machines think?" remains as pertinent as ever, offering a fertile ground for philosophical explorations. This inquiry, nestled at the intersection of technology and philosophy, prompts us to reassess our understanding of intelligence, consciousness, and the essence of being. It urges us to forge connections between the computational and the cognitive, the artificial and the natural, fostering a dialogue that seeks to unravel the complexities of mind and machine.

Thus, the voyage into the philosophical foundations of artificial intelligence remains a vibrant and evolving journey, a testament to human ingenuity and curiosity. It marks a quest to understand the depths of human cognition and the possibilities of replicating these faculties in machines. As we stand at this juncture, the explorations into the philosophical underpinnings of AI serve not just as a testament to technological advancements, but as a mirror reflecting humanity's eternal pursuit of understanding the intricacies of existence, intelligence, and the cosmos.

As we navigate this complex landscape, we may find that the answer to the question "Can machines think?" is not just a validation of technological prowess but a beacon guiding us to a deeper understanding of ourselves, an insight into the multifaceted nature of intelligence, and a glimpse into the potential futures that lie at the nexus of human and machine cognition. It is a question that invites us to ponder, explore, and perhaps redefine the contours of thought itself, fostering a journey that traverses through the realms of philosophy, technology, and perhaps, the unknown territories of a new intellectual frontier.

Alan Turing and the Turing Test

At the cradle of modern computing and artificial intelligence stands a figure whose intellect and foresight laid the foundations for the digital era that envelops us today: Alan Turing. A mathematician, logician, and wartime codebreaker, Turing is a man whose myriad contributions span across various disciplines, carving out an immortal niche in the annals of science and technology. The Turing Test is a pivotal part of his legacy, a theoretical construct that has governed the discourse surrounding artificial intelligence for more than half a century. In delving into Turing's life and works and the Turing Test's philosophical underpinning, we embark on a journey that interweaves human ingenuity with the relentless pursuit of mimicking human intelligence in machines.

From an early age, Alan Turing, born in 1912 in London, displayed an affinity for numbers and science. His educational journey was marked by a bias towards mathematics and logic, fields where he would later make monumental contributions. Turing's early career saw him delving into the realms of mathematical logic, with his 1936 paper on computable numbers presenting the concept of a universal machine capable of solving any computable problem. This theoretical construct laid the blueprint for modern computers, heralding the onset of the computing revolution that would engulf the world in the latter half of the 20th century.

But it was during the dark days of World War II that Turing's genius was pressed into service in a manner that would profoundly impact the course of history. At Bletchley Park, Britain's codebreaking centre, Turing played a vital role in deciphering encrypted German messages, a feat that required not only mathematical brilliance but also the creation of machines capable of sifting through a myriad of possible solutions at speeds unimaginable to human calculators. The work done at Bletchley Park remained shrouded in secrecy for many years, but today, it stands as a testament to Turing's multidisciplinary genius, a convergence of mathematics, linguistics, and what we would now recognize as computer science.

As the war ended, Turing shifted his focus toward the burgeoning field of machine intelligence. During this period, he conceptualized the Turing Test, a theoretical framework to evaluate machine intelligence. In a world still nascent to the nuances of computing, Turing proposed a remarkably forward-thinking question: "Can machines think?" Instead of entangling this query with debates on consciousness and cognition, Turing pragmatically shifted the focus towards observable behavior, theorizing that a machine could be said to be intelligent when it could imitate a human to the point that a judge could not distinguish between them based on their responses to questions.

The Turing Test, introduced in his 1950 paper titled "Computing Machinery and Intelligence," sparked a revolutionary discourse in the scientific community. It challenged the existing notions of machine capabilities and nudged humanity towards contemplating the possibilities of creating artificial beings with cognitive faculties. The Turing Test essentially proposed an operational definition of intelligence, divorcing the evaluation of machine intelligence from biological constraints and focusing on functional capabilities. This was a groundbreaking perspective, urging the world to consider the potential of machines to mimic human cognition, irrespective of the underlying mechanisms.

The Turing Test has since become a cornerstone in artificial intelligence, fostering a race to create machines capable of passing this test. It has ignited imaginations, spawning a multitude of research endeavors aiming to sculpt machines that can think, learn, and possibly, understand. Yet, this test is not without its criticisms. Many argue it sets a low bar for machine intelligence, focusing on surface-level imitation rather than genuine understanding and cognition. Philosophers and AI researchers alike have pointed out that a machine might be able to simulate human conversation convincingly without any real comprehension or consciousness.

Indeed, the philosophical implications of the Turing Test are vast, opening up avenues for discussion on consciousness, self-awareness, and the very essence of being. It contemplates whether mimicking human behavior and thought processes through computational means would grant machines a form of 'life' or whether they would remain soulless automatons, expertly imitating yet never truly embodying the richness of human experience.

As we delve deeper into the legacy of the Turing Test, we find it interlaced with broader philosophical inquiries that trace back to ancient civilizations. These inquiries touch upon metaphysical debates concerning mind and matter, challenging us to reconsider our definitions of life, intelligence, and consciousness in light of technological advancements. The Turing Test, thus, serves as a beacon, illuminating the intricate pathways that weave through the landscapes of science, philosophy, and technology, fostering a journey of exploration and discovery in the quest to understand the potentialities and limitations of artificial intelligence.

The legacy of Alan Turing and the Turing Test is monumental, reverberating through time and echoing the advancements that define the modern era. Turing's life, marked by brilliance and tragedy, is a beacon of human ingenuity and the relentless pursuit of knowledge. His untimely death in 1954, under circumstances that reflect the societal prejudices of the time, casts a somber shadow over his legacy. Yet, it is a legacy that refuses to be dimmed, shining brightly as a guiding light in artificial intelligence and beyond.

As we stand at the threshold of an era where machines are becoming increasingly integrated into our lives, the questions and hypotheses Turing posited become more relevant with each passing day. The Turing Test remains a significant milestone, a measure of humanity's progress in sculpting machines in our image. It stands as a testament to Turing's visionary approach, urging us to continually push the boundaries of what is deemed possible and to forge ahead in the quest to understand the intricate tapestry of intelligence, whether biological or artificial.

In conclusion, the journey through the life and works of Alan Turing and the philosophical exploration of the Turing Test invites us to ponder upon the complexities of intelligence and the potentials of artificial intelligence. It beckons us to envision a future where machines might not only think but possibly embody facets of consciousness, fostering a world where the boundaries between artificial and natural blur, ushering in an era of unprecedented collaboration and innovation. As we continue this voyage of discovery, the spirit of Alan Turing guides us, urging us to look beyond the horizons of the known, to dream, to explore, and to create. It is a journey that promises technological advancements and a deeper understanding of the intricacies of human cognition and the exploration of uncharted realms of intelligence and consciousness.

Early AI research:
The Dartmouth Workshop and the birth of AI as a discipline

In the annals of technological advancements and scientific exploration, few events are as pivotal as the Dartmouth Workshop, a meeting that signaled the nascent stages of what would eventually burgeon into the multifaceted discipline of Artificial Intelligence (AI). This workshop convened during the summer of 1956 at Dartmouth College, a hub of intellectual ferment, brought together a cohort of brilliant minds who envisioned a future where machines could potentially mimic human intelligence. This seminal event can be likened to a crucible, where theories converged and crystallized to give birth to AI as a structured field of inquiry. Herein, we traverse the intricate tapestry of early AI research, with the Dartmouth Workshop serving as our focal point, a beacon illuminating the dawn of a new scientific era.

The origins of artificial intelligence as a scientific discipline are deeply rooted in the intellectual currents of the mid-20th century. During this period, the worlds of mathematics, logic, psychology, and engineering were undergoing significant transformations, paving the way for a convergence that would bring forth the multifaceted field of AI. The seeds for this convergence were sown by pioneers like Alan Turing, who introduced the concept of machine intelligence and laid the groundwork for computational theory. As the 1950s rolled in, the stage was set for a gathering of minds that would formally usher in the era of artificial intelligence research.

It was against this vibrant backdrop that the Dartmouth Workshop was conceived. Proposed by John McCarthy, Marvin Minsky, Nathaniel Rochester, and Claude Shannon, all stalwarts in their respective fields, the workshop was predicated on the belief that "every aspect of learning or any other feature of intelligence can in principle be so precisely described that a machine can be made to simulate it." This ambitious proposition became the cornerstone of the Dartmouth conference, seeking to bridge the gap between machines and human intelligence, fostering a dialogue that would shape the contours of AI research for decades to come.

As the summer of 1956 unfurled, Dartmouth College became the epicenter of intellectual discourse on machine intelligence. The workshop convened a group of scholars with diverse backgrounds, including the proposers and prominent figures such as Trenchard More and Arthur Samuel. For eight weeks, these brilliant minds engaged in a vibrant exchange of ideas, tackling complex questions surrounding the capabilities of machines and the potential to replicate human cognitive processes through computational means.

The Dartmouth Workshop served as a fertile ground where foundational theories in AI began to take shape. One of the significant outcomes of this meeting was the crystallization of the term "Artificial Intelligence," coined by John McCarthy, which encapsulated the essence of the discipline - the creation of machine entities endowed with intelligence that could potentially mirror human cognition. This marked a decisive shift from merely viewing machines as tools to envisioning them as entities capable of learning, reasoning, and perhaps, understanding.

Furthermore, the workshop fostered research into various facets of AI, catalyzing developments in natural language processing, neural networks, and cognitive simulation. It engendered a belief in the feasibility of creating intelligent machines, fueling research endeavors that sought to push the boundaries of what machines could achieve. During these deliberations, concepts that would later become central to AI research, such as machine learning and problem-solving, were nurtured, setting the stage for the rapid advancements that would follow in subsequent decades.

However, the Dartmouth Workshop was not just a platform for theoretical discussions. It also witnessed the genesis of concrete projects to bring AI theories to life. Participants engaged in hands-on work, developing early AI programs that sought to embody the principles discussed during the conference. These initial endeavors, albeit rudimentary by modern standards, were revolutionary for their time, breaking new ground in applying computational techniques to mimic human-like intelligence.

As we delve deeper into the intricacies of the Dartmouth Workshop, it becomes evident that this event marked a watershed moment in the history of technology and science. It transformed AI from a concept relegated to the realms of science fiction to a legitimate field of academic inquiry and research. The workshop served as a crucible where ideas converged and synergized, giving birth to a discipline that promised redefining human-machine interaction boundaries.

Yet, the Dartmouth Workshop was not without its critics. The bold assertions made during the conference were met with skepticism, with detractors questioning the feasibility of replicating the complexities of human intelligence in machines. The workshop's ambitious scope ignited debates on the philosophical implications of AI, fostering discussions on the nature of consciousness, the essence of intelligence, and the ethical considerations surrounding the creation of intelligent machines. These debates, ignited during the early days of AI research, continue to reverberate in contemporary discourse, shaping the narrative surrounding the advancements and limitations of AI technology.

Moreover, the Dartmouth Workshop paved the way for establishing AI as a formalized discipline within the academic sphere. In the years following the workshop, AI research centers began sprouting in various institutions, fostering an environment that nurtured innovation and exploration in artificial intelligence. The workshop ignited a flame that would continue to burn brightly, inspiring generations of researchers to delve into the fascinating world of AI and fostering a journey of discovery that sought to unravel the mysteries of intelligence and cognition.

Looking back, it is evident that the Dartmouth Workshop served as a beacon, illuminating the path for the burgeoning field of artificial intelligence. It marked the confluence of diverse streams of thought, fostering a collaborative environment that catalyzed the birth of AI as a structured discipline. The workshop stood as a testament to human ingenuity and the relentless pursuit of knowledge, embodying the spirit of exploration that lies at the heart of scientific endeavor.

In conclusion, the Dartmouth Workshop is a monumental milestone in the artificial intelligence journey. It marked the dawn of a new era, where the boundaries between man and machine began to blur, ushering in a world of limitless possibilities and potential. As we navigate the complex landscape of modern AI, the echoes of the Dartmouth Workshop reverberate, reminding us of the vibrant beginnings of a field that promises to redefine the future of humanity. Through the lens of this historic event, we witness the birth of a discipline that has captivated imaginations and ignited debates, fostering a journey that traverses the realms of science, technology, and philosophy. It serves as a foundation stone, upon which the edifice of artificial intelligence has been built, fostering a legacy that continues to shape the narrative of human progress in the digital age.

CHAPTER II

Fundamental Concepts in AI

Definitions: Narrow AI vs. General AI

In the evolving glossary of the technology world, the terms "Narrow AI" and "General AI" have carved significant niches, representing two distinct approaches and philosophies in developing and implementing artificial intelligence. These terms demarcate a clear boundary between machines programmed to excel in specific tasks and those envisioned to have cognitive abilities spanning a breadth akin to human intelligence. In this section, we shall journey through these terms' intricate landscapes, exploring their meanings, implications, and the significant strides humanity has made in each domain.

Since its conceptual inception, Artificial Intelligence has been a field of endless possibilities and potential. It represents the intersection of science and philosophy, where machines are viewed as tools and entities capable of learning and possibly understanding. This dynamic field continually presents two discernible paths, each with its philosophies and methodologies: Narrow AI, also known as Weak AI, and General AI, also referred to as Strong AI. These two paradigms embody the divergent approaches to imbuing machines with intelligence, and in doing so, signify different horizons of achievement and aspiration.

Narrow AI, as the name suggests, focuses on developing artificial intelligence systems with limited capabilities. These systems are adept at performing specific tasks, often outperforming humans in speed and accuracy. In the domain of Narrow AI, machines are trained to excel in designated areas, be it data analysis, image recognition, or language translation. This segment of AI is marked by a high degree of specialization, where algorithms are tailored to suit particular tasks, honing them to perfection through relentless iterations and refinements.

Narrow AI is pervasive in the contemporary world, seamlessly integrating into various aspects of daily life. Narrow AI has been a transformative force, from voice-activated assistants to recommendation systems on e-commerce platforms, reshaping industries and altering consumer behaviors. These AI systems, confined to their realms of expertise, function within defined parameters, mastering the art of executing their designated tasks with unparalleled precision. However, the scope of Narrow AI is circumscribed, confined to the boundaries of its programming and unable to venture beyond the territories of generalized understanding and cognition.

On the other hand, General AI embodies a vision that transcends the confines of specialized task execution. This realm of AI aspires to create machines endowed with a breadth of understanding and cognition akin to human intelligence. This ambitious venture aims to develop artificial entities capable of learning, adapting, and understanding a wide array of tasks, not limited to a specific domain. General AI represents the pinnacle of artificial intelligence, where machines would potentially possess the ability to understand, reason, and interact with the world in a manner indistinguishable from human beings.

The world of General AI is marked by a complexity that mirrors the intricacies of the human mind. Here, machines are not confined to scripted responses or predefined algorithms but are envisioned to possess the ability to think, learn, and evolve, navigating through an ever-changing environment with a deep and wide understanding. Therefore, the development of General AI involves grappling with questions that are as much philosophical as they are technological, delving into the mysteries of consciousness, cognition, and the essence of intelligence.

The pursuit of General AI has been a journey of innovation and discovery, where researchers and scientists venture into uncharted territories to unravel the secrets of human intelligence and replicate them in machines. This journey is marked by trials and tribulations, where the complexities of human cognition present formidable challenges, pushing the boundaries of technology and knowledge. Yet, this pursuit embodies the spirit of human ingenuity, reflecting the relentless quest for knowledge and understanding that has defined the human experience throughout history.

At this juncture, exploring the implications and potential trajectories of these two paradigms is pertinent. With its specialized focus, the domain of Narrow AI has proven to be immensely beneficial, driving advancements in various sectors including healthcare, finance, and entertainment. Its applications are myriad, offering solutions that enhance efficiency and facilitate innovation. However, the journey of Narrow AI is one of incremental advancements, where each step forward is confined to a specific domain, offering improvements and refinements within that sphere.

Contrarily, the voyage into the world of General AI is marked by an aspiration to leap beyond the incremental advancements, to forge a future where machines could potentially possess a holistic understanding of the world, akin to human beings. This vision of AI represents a frontier that is both exciting and daunting, where the possibilities are boundless, offering glimpses into a future where the boundaries between humans and machines blur, fostering collaboration and synergy that could reshape the fabric of society and redefine the notion of intelligence.

As we stand at the threshold of a new era, the discourse surrounding Narrow and General AI takes on a heightened significance. The ethical considerations surrounding AI development, particularly in the realm of General AI, come to the fore, fostering debates on the implications of creating machines with potentially sentient capabilities. These discussions traverse the domains of philosophy, ethics, and sociology, engaging with questions surrounding autonomy, consciousness, and the potential for artificial entities to possess rights and responsibilities.

In conclusion, the journey through the landscapes of Narrow AI and General AI offers a panoramic view of a field in a dynamic evolution state. These two paradigms, representing distinct philosophies and approaches, embody the diversity and complexity of artificial intelligence as a discipline. As we navigate through the nuances of Narrow and General AI, we are invited to ponder upon the potentials and challenges that lie ahead, to envision a future where technology and humanity merge in a symbiotic relationship, fostering a world marked by innovation, collaboration, and an expanded understanding of intelligence and consciousness. The road ahead is one of exploration and discovery, where the boundaries of knowledge are pushed, and the horizons of possibility expanded, fostering a journey that promises to redefine the contours of human existence in the digital age.

Machine Learning: A brief introduction

In the sprawling panorama of artificial intelligence, machine learning emerges as a critical subsection, a domain where technology's aspirations converge with data science's sophistication. It represents a foray into an era where machines not only compute but learn, evolve, and adapt to the ever-changing dynamics of the modern world. In this section, we will go on an exploratory journey into machine learning, offering a concise yet comprehensive introduction to a field that stands at the vanguard of technological innovation and progression.

Fundamentally, machine learning is an area of artificial intelligence focused on creating models and algorithms that let computers see patterns and decide for themselves without needing to be specifically taught to do so. It is similar to sowing seeds in fertile soil, where the seeds represent algorithms and the soil symbolizes the rich and diverse data landscape. These seeds, once planted, grow and adapt to the contours of the data environment, evolving into intelligent entities capable of discerning patterns, recognizing trends, and offering insights that transcend the capabilities of traditional computational methods.

Historically, the roots of machine learning stretch back to the mid-20th century, intertwining with the broader developments in artificial intelligence. Early endeavors in this domain were guided by the aspiration to create machines that could mimic the learning capabilities of the human brain, a venture that sought to bridge the gap between man and machine. As the decades rolled on, machine learning began to crystallize as a distinct field, marked by the convergence of statistics, computer science, and mathematics. These interdisciplinary interactions laid the foundation for developing algorithms that could learn from and interpret data, forging a new pathway in the artificial intelligence journey.

In the modern context, machine learning is characterized by a dynamic and multifaceted landscape where numerous techniques and methodologies coalesce to create systems that are adept at learning from data. Supervised learning, a prominent approach in machine learning, involves training models using labeled data, where the model learns to map inputs to outputs, gradually refining its predictions as it is exposed to more data. This process is akin to a teacher-student interaction, where the model learns under the guidance of a teacher, represented by the labeled data.

On the other hand, unsupervised learning ventures into the realm of discovery, where models are tasked with uncovering hidden patterns and structures in unlabeled data. This approach is characterized by an exploratory spirit, where the model navigates through the data landscape, seeking to identify clusters, associations, and underlying patterns that offer insights into the intrinsic characteristics of the data.

Semi-supervised learning, a hybrid approach, combines supervised and unsupervised learning elements, utilizing a mix of labeled and unlabeled data to train models. This methodology seeks to harness the strengths of both approaches, fostering a learning environment that is both guided and exploratory, offering a nuanced and balanced perspective on data analysis.

As we delve deeper into the world of machine learning, we encounter the fascinating domain of reinforcement learning, a technique that is inspired by behavioral psychology, where models learn to interact with their environment to achieve specific goals. In this approach, the learning process is driven by a system of rewards and punishments, where the model learns through trial and error, constantly adapting and evolving to optimize its performance.

In recent years, machine learning has also been enriched by the advent of deep learning, a subset that draws inspiration from the human brain's neural networks. Deep learning models, characterized by their layered architectures, can process complex, high-dimensional data, offering deep and nuanced insights. This approach has catalyzed significant advancements in fields such as image and speech recognition, revolutionizing the ways in which machines interact with the world.

In the contemporary landscape, machine learning stands as a beacon of innovation, offering solutions that are transforming industries and reshaping societal norms. From healthcare to finance, machine learning applications are myriad, providing tools that enhance efficiency, foster innovation, and drive progress. These developments are characterized by a synergy between man and machine, where the capabilities of machines are harnessed to augment human intelligence, fostering a collaborative environment that promises to redefine the contours of the modern world.

However, the journey of machine learning is also marked by challenges and considerations that warrant attention. As we venture further into this domain, data privacy, security, and ethics questions come to the fore. The deployment of machine learning models necessitates carefully evaluating the potential implications, fostering a discourse grounded in the principles of responsibility and ethical stewardship. Moreover, the complexities of machine learning also present challenges in terms of computational resources, data quality, and model interpretability, which require ongoing research and innovation to address.

In conclusion, machine learning represents a vibrant and dynamic field, where the aspirations of technology converge with the sophistication of data science. It embodies a journey of discovery and innovation, where machines evolve from mere calculators to entities capable of learning and adaptation. As we stand at the threshold of a new era, machine learning offers a glimpse into a future where the boundaries between humans and machines blur, fostering a symbiotic relationship that promises to usher in a new age of progress and discovery. Through the lens of machine learning, we witness the unfolding of a narrative marked by collaboration, innovation, and an expanded understanding of the complexities of the modern world. It beckons us to envision a future where technology catalyzes progress, driving humanity forward into a realm of unlimited potential and possibility.

The role of data in AI

In the pulsating heartbeat of the technological renaissance, the phrase' data is the new oil' echoes with resonant truth, denoting data's critical role in fueling the engines of artificial intelligence (AI). Data is the pillar upon which AI systems are built, providing the raw material that drives learning, innovation, and decision-making in an ever-increasing automated world. In this section, we delve into the intricate relationship between data and AI, exploring the myriad ways in which data serves as the cornerstone of AI developments and applications.

To appreciate fully the gravity of data's role in AI, one must first understand the fundamental principles that govern AI's functionality. Artificial Intelligence, in essence, refers to the development of computer systems that mimic human intelligence processes such as learning, reasoning, and problem-solving. These systems are designed to process huge amounts of data, learning to identify patterns and making predictions or decisions based on the analyzed information. Thus, data serves as the linchpin that anchors the operations of AI, facilitating the transformation of raw information into actionable insights and knowledge.

The symbiotic relationship between data and AI can be visualized as a dynamic cycle of input and output, where data serves as the input that feeds AI systems and the output generated through AI's analytical processes. This cycle starts with data acquisition, gathering vast information from various sources, including sensors, digital platforms, and public repositories. This initial phase lays the foundation for the subsequent stages, providing the raw material that fuels the analytical engines of AI.

Once the data is acquired, it undergoes a process of cleaning and preprocessing to ensure its quality and reliability. This step is vital in ensuring the accuracy and effectiveness of AI systems, as the quality of the input data directly impacts the output quality. Data cleansing involves the removal of inconsistencies, inaccuracies, and noise, creating a refined dataset primed for analysis.

Following the preprocessing phase, the data enters the analytical crucible of AI, where it is subjected to a range of techniques and methodologies designed to extract meaningful insights. This process, known as data mining, employs a variety of algorithms and statistical techniques to identify patterns, trends, and relationships within the data. Machine learning, a subset of AI, plays a pivotal role in this stage, utilizing algorithms that learn and improve over time, honing their ability to analyze and interpret data with increasing sophistication.

Deep learning, an area of machine learning inspired by the neural networks present in the human brain, is arguably the best example of the transformative power of data in artificial intelligence. Here, data undergoes a process of hierarchical analysis, where complex patterns are decomposed into simpler representations through a series of layered networks. These networks, trained on vast datasets, develop the ability to recognize intricate patterns, enabling the creation of AI systems capable of tasks such as image and speech recognition, natural language processing (NLP), and autonomous vehicle navigation.

As AI systems continue to evolve, the role of data expands to encompass a range of functionalities that extend beyond the analytical sphere. Data now serves as a model validation and optimization tool, where AI systems are tested and refined using separate datasets to ensure their performance and reliability. Moreover, data plays a critical role in developing AI-powered predictive models, which leverage historical data to make forecasts about future events, aiding in decision-making and strategy formulation across various sectors including finance, healthcare, and marketing.

Furthermore, data holds the key to unlocking the potential of AI in the domain of personalized services and products. Through the analysis of user data, AI systems can tailor their offerings to meet consumers' individual preferences and needs, fostering a new era of personalized experiences that transcend the capabilities of traditional methods.

However, the omnipresence of data in the modern world raises pressing concerns regarding privacy, security, and ethical considerations. The proliferation of data-driven AI systems necessitates the development of robust frameworks that safeguard the rights and privacy of individuals, ensuring that data is handled with the utmost responsibility and ethical integrity. This aspect underscores the importance of fostering a culture of data literacy and awareness, where individuals as well as organizations are equipped with the knowledge and tools to navigate the complex data landscape with discernment and caution.

Moreover, the role of data in AI brings to light the critical issue of data bias, where AI systems may inherit the biases present in the training data, leading to skewed and discriminatory outcomes. Addressing this issue requires concerted efforts to develop unbiased data collection methods and the implementation of mechanisms that detect and mitigate bias in AI systems, fostering a landscape of inclusivity and fairness.

In conclusion, the role of data in AI represents a dynamic and multifaceted relationship, characterized by a continuous cycle of input and output that drives the operations and developments in the AI sphere. Data is the cornerstone of AI, facilitating the transformation of raw information into actionable insights and knowledge. It fosters innovation, personalization, and predictive capabilities, reshaping the landscape of technology and society.

As we stand at the cusp of a new era, the intertwined destinies of data and AI beckon us to envision a future where technology and humanity merge in a harmonious symbiosis, fueled by the power of data. It calls upon us to navigate the complex data landscape with responsibility, ethics, and a vision that aims to harness the potential of AI for the betterment of society. Through the lens of data, we witness the unfolding narrative of AI, a journey marked by discovery, innovation, and the relentless pursuit of knowledge, promising to usher humanity into a new age of prosperity and progress, guided by the beacon of data-driven intelligence.

Algorithms and Neural Networks

In the grand mosaic of artificial intelligence (AI), algorithms and neural networks manifest as quintessential components, intricately woven to shape modern computing intelligence's intricate tapestry. These two intertwined concepts are not only central to the functioning of AI but also epitomize the breathtaking strides technology has taken to emulate the intricacies of human cognition and learning. In this section, we shall traverse through the labyrinthine pathways of algorithms and neural networks, elucidating their characteristics, intricacies, and the role they play in bringing the vision of artificial intelligence to fruition.

To begin our expedition, we ought to cast a spotlight on algorithms, the fundamental building blocks of any computational process. In its essence, an algorithm is a finite set of instructions formulated to solve a specific problem. This mathematical concept has found applications in various domains long before the advent of computers. However, with the inception of computational technology, algorithms have metamorphosed into sophisticated entities capable of tackling intricate tasks with remarkable efficiency and precision. Their structured approach, encompassing well-defined steps and rules, facilitates the systematic analysis and processing of data, enabling computers to execute complex functions seamlessly.

In the context of AI, algorithms adopt a pivotal role, orchestrating a symphony of operations that underpin the intelligence of machines. These entities are harnessed to create models that can learn and adapt, morphing into dynamic tools that evolve with experience. Machine learning, a subset of AI, exemplifies the application of algorithms to facilitate the learning process of computers. Here, algorithms navigate through a sea of data, identifying patterns, making predictions, and refining their accuracy with each iteration. This iterative process echoes the evolutionary nature of learning, where experience fosters growth and refinement.

As we venture further into the world of AI, we encounter the mesmerizing realm of neural networks, a concept inspired by the complex structure of the human brain. Neural networks represent a paradigm shift in computational techniques, moving away from linear models to adopt a more holistic, interconnected approach to data processing. This network comprises layers of nodes, analogous to neurons in the human brain, interconnected through synapses that transmit signals across the network.

In a neural network, the intricacies of human cognition are mirrored in the structured yet flexible architecture that allows for complex, non-linear data processing. At the heart of this network lies the learning process, where algorithms are used to adjust the weights of the connections between nodes, optimizing the network's performance in predicting or classifying data. The nodes are organized into layers: the input layer, which receives the initial data; one or more hidden layers, where the data is processed; and the output layer, where the final result is produced.

Deep learning, a further specialization within the domain of neural networks, employs multi-layered networks to facilitate the analysis of high-dimensional data. In these deep neural networks, the multitude of layers allows for extracting progressively more abstract features from the input data. This hierarchical approach to learning enables deep learning models to excel in tasks such as image and speech recognition, where the ability to identify complex patterns and relationships is paramount.

As we navigate the landscape of neural networks, we stumble upon various specialized structures, each tailored to address specific problems. Convolutional Neural Networks (CNNs), for instance, have proven to be highly efficient in image recognition tasks, utilizing layers with convolutional filters that can identify spatial patterns in data. Recurrent Neural Networks (RNNs), on the other hand, excel in processing sequential data, incorporating loops within the network that allow for the retention of information over time, making them apt for tasks such as language modeling and time series analysis.

Yet, in this ocean of complexities, the marriage between algorithms and neural networks is not devoid of challenges. The intricate structures and computations can sometimes morph into a web of obscurity, making it difficult to interpret the decision-making process of these models. This lack of transparency, often called the "black box" phenomenon, raises concerns regarding the accountability and reliability of AI systems, especially in critical applications where understanding the decision-making process is crucial.

Furthermore, developing and optimizing algorithms and neural networks require substantial computational resources and expertise. The training of deep neural networks, mainly, necessitates vast amounts of data and computing power, sometimes restricting the feasibility of these models to organizations with significant resources. Moreover, the ethical implications of data usage and algorithmic decision-making beckon a cautious and responsible approach to developing and deploying AI systems, fostering a discourse that emphasizes fairness, transparency, and ethical stewardship.

In conclusion, as we stand at the intersection of technology and cognition, algorithms and neural networks emerge as beacon lights guiding us into a future steeped in intelligence and automation. These elements embody the fusion of mathematical precision and biological inspiration, crafting a narrative where machines are not mere calculators but entities capable of learning, evolving, and possibly understanding.

As we forge ahead into this brave new world, we are called upon to navigate the intricacies of this journey with a discerning eye, fostering a harmony between innovation and ethical responsibility. Through the lens of algorithms and neural networks, we glimpse the contours of a future where the boundaries between man and machine blur, giving rise to a symbiotic existence that promises to redefine the essence of intelligence, creativity, and innovation.

Thus, the exploration of algorithms and neural networks serves not just as a testament to human ingenuity but also as a canvas, where the vibrant hues of technology blend with the nuanced strokes of human cognition, crafting a masterpiece that resonates with the harmonious symphony of progress, discovery, and unbounded potential.

CHAPTER III

Milestones in AI Development

Game playing: Deep Blue and Chess, AlphaGo and Go

At the intersection of technology and intellect, the chronicles of game-playing machines, such as Deep Blue and AlphaGo, stand as epochal narratives illustrating the burgeoning prowess of artificial intelligence (AI). These magnificent milestones heralded the age of machines capable of mastering complex games historically dominated by human intellect and ignited profound conversations about the depth and breadth of machine learning and computational capability. In this section, we embark on a journey through time, delving into the tales of Deep Blue's conquest in the realm of chess and AlphaGo's mastery over the ancient game of Go, exploring the nuances, technologies, and the groundbreaking implications they brought to the world of artificial intelligence and beyond.

The narrative commences with Deep Blue, a titan forged in the laboratories of IBM during the mid-1990s, embodying the pinnacle of computational power and algorithmic prowess of its time. In the serene yet intense milieu of the chess board, Deep Blue embarked on a mission to dethrone the reigning monarch of the chess world,

Grandmaster Garry Kasparov. This clash between man and machine played out on the 64 squares of the chess board, represented much more than a game; it was a testament to the crescendo of artificial intelligence, seeking to reach unparalleled heights of cognitive capability.

Deep Blue, a behemoth grounded in the principles of brute force computation, wielded its prowess to evaluate millions of positions per second, a feat unachievable by the human mind. Its strategy hinged on a combination of raw computational power and a vast database of chess knowledge amassed from historical games and strategic formulations. Deep Blue's architecture was designed to delve deep into the tree of possible moves, employing sophisticated evaluation functions to analyze and select the most potent strategies.

The saga reached its zenith in 1997 when the silence of the chess hall echoed with the unprecedented triumph of machine over man. Deep Blue managed to conquer Kasparov, marking the first instance where a computer system triumphed over a World Chess Champion under standard chess tournament time controls. This victory not only shattered the veneer of human superiority in chess but also sparked widespread intrigue and contemplation on the potential boundaries of artificial intelligence.

However, the realm of artificial intelligence was not destined to halt its march at the bastions of chess. Nearly two decades later, the world witnessed the emergence of another prodigious entity, AlphaGo, nurtured in the innovative corridors of DeepMind

Technologies. This new frontier sought to conquer the ancient Chinese game of Go, a pursuit characterized by its profound complexity and an astronomical number of possible board configurations, dwarfing even that of chess. The game of Go, revered for centuries as a bastion of strategic depth and intellectual prowess, presented a monumental challenge for artificial intelligence.

To navigate the labyrinthine complexities of Go, AlphaGo was forged with a blend of cutting-edge technologies, transcending the brute force approach that characterized its predecessor, Deep Blue. At its core, AlphaGo leveraged the power of neural networks and machine learning, employing a combination of Monte Carlo Tree Search (or MCTS) and deep neural networks to analyze and predict potential moves. Its neural networks, trained on a vast repository of games, honed the ability to evaluate board positions and strategize moves with a depth of understanding that blurred the lines between artificial and human intelligence.

AlphaGo's deep learning approach allowed it to learn and evolve, assimilating the game's nuances with each iteration. Moreover, AlphaGo was trained through reinforcement learning, a method wherein the program continuously played millions of games against itself, learning to refine its strategies and tactics. This ability to learn and adapt imbued AlphaGo with creativity, enabling it to devise novel strategies and moves that startled and fascinated Go enthusiasts and experts alike.

In 2016, the world witnessed a historic confrontation between AlphaGo and Lee Sedol, a grandmaster in the realm of Go. This monumental event unfurled over a series of games that showed AlphaGo demonstrating skill, strategy, and foresight that captivated the global audience. Its triumph over Lee Sedol was not just a victory in the conventional sense but a demonstration of the transformative potential of artificial intelligence, capable of surmounting complexities that were hitherto considered the exclusive domain of human intellect.

The victories of Deep Blue and AlphaGo reverberate far beyond the boundaries of game boards, marking seminal moments in the evolutionary journey of artificial intelligence. These accomplishments ignited philosophical debates and contemplations on the nature of intelligence, creativity, and the future trajectory of human-machine symbiosis. Furthermore, the technologies and methodologies nurtured in the crucible of game-playing AI found resonance in myriad other domains, fostering innovations in healthcare, logistics, finance, and numerous other fields.

Yet, amidst the exhilaration of these victories, one cannot overlook the introspective reflections they engender. These confrontations between man and machine beckon society to ponder upon the ethical dimensions, the implications for human identity and the trajectory of artificial intelligence. As we stand at the cusp of an era where artificial intelligence promises to redefine the paradigms of innovation and cognition, these games mirror the potential futures that await humanity.

In conclusion, the sagas of Deep Blue and AlphaGo emerge as poetic narratives in the odyssey of artificial intelligence. They stand as luminous beacons illuminating the path of technological evolution, where machines metamorphose into entities capable of intellectual depth and strategic mastery. These tales encapsulate the harmonious dance between technology and intellect, weaving a tapestry that illustrates the symbiotic potential of human and artificial intelligence.

As we navigate the unfolding narrative of the 21st century, the legacies of Deep Blue and AlphaGo serve as both inspiration and a gentle caution. They beckon us to foster a future where technology and humanity coalesce in a symphony of mutual growth and enrichment. A future where artificial intelligence transcends its role as a mere tool, evolving into a partner that complements the human spirit in its relentless pursuit of knowledge, understanding, and the exploration of the boundless vistas of potential that lie before us.

Natural language processing: Chatbots and translators

In the vast and ever-evolving frontier of artificial intelligence, natural language processing (NLP) emerges as a luminous constellation that exemplifies the delicate confluence of linguistics and computational prowess. This dazzling intersection has given birth to remarkably intuitive technologies such as chatbots and translators, which have seamlessly integrated into our daily interactions, revolutionizing how we communicate and comprehend languages. In this section, we shall delve into the intricate world of NLP, emphasizing the marvels of chatbots and translators, the technologies that underpin them, and their transformative impact on contemporary society.

Embarking on our exploration, we must first understand the nuanced canvas of natural language processing. At its core, NLP is a field of AI that strives to facilitate the seamless interaction between humans and computers using natural language. This discipline extends its roots deep into linguistics, computer science, and artificial intelligence, aiming to enable machines to comprehend, respond, and generate human language in a valuable manner. The challenges in this realm are manifold, as it seeks to navigate the labyrinthine pathways of human language, characterized by its complex syntax, semantics, and ever-evolving nuances. Despite these challenges, advancements in machine learning and computational power have fueled significant strides in NLP, ushering in an era of intelligent systems that engage in rich and nuanced language-based interactions.

In this blossoming garden of NLP, chatbots emerge as vibrant blossoms, embodying the interactive facet of natural language processing. Chatbots, or conversational agents, are designed to simulate human conversation, capable of engaging with users through text-based or voice-based mediums. In the embryonic stages, chatbots were largely rule-based, relying on predefined scripts and patterns to interact with users. However, as the sands of time flowed, chatbots have metamorphosed into sophisticated entities, harnessing the power of machine learning and deep learning to comprehend and generate language with an unprecedented depth of understanding.

In the modern landscape, chatbots are fueled by various technologies that facilitate nuanced and dynamic conversations. These include sentiment analysis, which enables the chatbot to gauge the emotional tone of the conversation, and entity recognition, which assists in identifying and extracting pertinent information from the user's input. Moreover, contemporary chatbots employ deep learning models, including recurrent neural networks (RNNs) and transformer models, which allow them to analyze and generate language in a contextually rich and coherent manner.

These technological advancements have empowered chatbots to play various roles across various sectors. In customer service, chatbots are diligent assistants, available round the clock to address queries and provide information. In healthcare, chatbots are harnessed as virtual health assistants, aiding in monitoring patient health and disseminating medical information. Furthermore, chatbots have found resonance in the educational sphere, functioning as intelligent tutors capable of providing personalized learning experiences. Through these roles, chatbots have streamlined processes and enriched the user experience, offering personalized and interactive avenues for engagement.

Parallelly, the realm of NLP unfurls another remarkable narrative in the form of translators, epitomizing the dream of breaking language barriers and fostering universal communication. The journey of machine translation has been marked by progressive phases, each characterized by increasing sophistication and linguistic depth. Initially grounded in rule-based systems, which relied heavily on linguistic rules and bilingual dictionaries, machine translation evolved to embrace statistical methods, utilizing statistical models to analyze bilingual corpora and generate translations.

The zenith of this evolution is witnessed in the emergence of neural machine translation, which leverages deep neural networks to facilitate translation processes. These networks, akin to the intricate neural circuits of the human brain, are adept at capturing the subtleties and intricacies of language, providing translations that resonate with a profound semantic depth and fluency. By analyzing vast repositories of bilingual data, neural machine translation systems can learn complex linguistic patterns and relationships, offering translations that are accurate, contextually rich, and coherent.

Moreover, these translation systems are bolstered by technologies such as attention mechanisms, which enable the model to concentrate on different parts of the input sequence when generating an output sequence, thereby enhancing the quality and relevance of the translation. Additionally, the advent of transformer models, characterized by their parallelization and scalability, has further augmented the capabilities of machine translators, enabling them to process language with remarkable speed and efficiency.

These advancements in machine translation have crafted a world where language barriers are gradually dissolving, facilitating seamless communication and interaction across linguistic boundaries. Machine translators serve as bridges in this interconnected global village, fostering understanding, collaboration, and cultural exchange. They have become indispensable tools in various domains, including business, education, and tourism, aiding in document translation, real-time interpretation, and language learning.

As we stand amidst this vibrant tapestry of natural language processing, we must acknowledge the transformative impact of chatbots and translators. These technologies embody the harmonious amalgamation of linguistic science and artificial intelligence, offering avenues for enriched and universal communication. They signify the dawn of an era where machines not only understand the intricacies of human language but also engage in meaningful and dynamic dialogues, fostering a world marked by inclusivity, understanding, and mutual respect.

Nevertheless, this journey is not devoid of challenges and contemplations. The complexities of human language, characterized by its contextual nuances, idiomatic expressions, and cultural variations, pose a continuous challenge to the field of NLP. Moreover, the ethical dimensions of language processing technologies beckon a conscientious approach, emphasizing the values of privacy, consent, and responsible AI development.

In conclusion, as we navigate through the mesmerizing narrative of natural language processing, we are witnesses to a revolution, one that is reshaping the contours of communication and interaction. Chatbots and translators stand as luminous beacons in this journey, illuminating the path toward a future where language is not a barrier but a conduit for understanding and collaboration. As we venture further into this narrative, we are called upon to foster a landscape where technology and language coalesce in a symphony of innovation, empathy, and universal harmony, crafting a world where artificial intelligence serves as a partner in the beautiful and complex dance of human communication and understanding.

Image recognition: From basic facial recognition to deepfakes

In the sprawling domain of artificial intelligence, the sector of image recognition stands as a field of awe-inspiring potential and intricate complexities. From its embryonic stages, primarily encompassing facial recognition technologies to its modern advancements, where deepfakes reside, image recognition has continually altered our interaction with digital realms and transformed societal paradigms. This section seeks to navigate through the labyrinthine journey of image recognition, discerning its evolution from fundamental facial recognition techniques to the emergence of deepfakes, a phenomenon that has challenged our perceptions of reality in the digital age.

At its genesis, image recognition technology was conceived as a tool to facilitate the identification and verification of individuals through facial analysis. The technology was relatively rudimentary in its initial stages, employing basic geometric algorithms to recognize facial features and patterns. These early systems relied heavily on the explicit programming of rules and were limited in their ability to accurately identify faces, especially in varying lighting conditions and angles. However, the foundations were laid, setting the stage for a revolutionary journey through the realms of technological evolution and innovation.

As time progressed, facial recognition technology evolved, embracing more sophisticated methods and algorithms. The transition from rule-based systems to machine learning marked a significant milestone in this evolution, facilitating a more nuanced and dynamic approach to image analysis. Machine learning algorithms, powered by the analysis of large datasets, enabled these systems to learn and adapt, enhancing their ability to accurately identify and verify faces through complex pattern recognition and feature extraction techniques. These advancements have propelled facial recognition technology into numerous applications, from security and surveillance to social media and consumer electronics, weaving it seamlessly into the fabric of modern society.

The metamorphosis of image recognition technology reached a new zenith with the advent of deep learning, an area of machine learning inspired by the human brain's neural networks. Deep learning algorithms, particularly convolutional neural networks (CNNs), have revolutionized the field of image recognition, providing the ability to analyze and interpret images with remarkable depth and accuracy. These networks are adept at extracting hierarchical features from images, allowing them to discern intricate patterns and relationships that were previously unattainable. Through deep learning, facial recognition technology has achieved unprecedented levels of accuracy and reliability, fostering a world where digital systems can interact with humans in increasingly intelligent and intuitive ways.

Yet, as we traverse further into this narrative, we encounter a phenomenon that stands as a testament to the double-edged nature of technological advancement: deepfakes. In the labyrinthine corridors of image recognition, deepfakes represent a dark alley, where the boundaries between reality and illusion blur, challenging our perceptions of truth and authenticity in the digital world.

Deepfakes, a term coined from "deep learning" and "fake," epitomize using deep learning techniques to create compelling forged videos and images. This technology hinges on the power of generative adversarial networks (or GANs), a class of artificial intelligence algorithms that employ two neural networks in a kind of cat-and-mouse game: one network strives to create increasingly convincing forgeries, while the other endeavors to detect these fabrications. Through this iterative process, the generative network continually refines its ability to create fakes, eventually producing nearly indistinguishable results from real images and videos.

The emergence of deepfakes has ushered us into an era where seeing is no longer believing. These highly convincing forgeries have the potential to manipulate narratives, distort truths, and sow discord, challenging the very foundations of trust and authenticity in the digital landscape. The implications are manifold and deeply concerning, spanning across various domains including politics, media, and entertainment. Deepfakes can be weaponized to create fraudulent content, spread misinformation, and undermine public trust, posing significant challenges to society and democracy.

Moreover, deepfakes have ignited profound ethical and moral debates, beckoning us to ponder the responsibilities and consequences associated with deploying advanced image recognition technologies. The potential misuse of deepfakes for nefarious purposes, such as creating non-consensual explicit content or perpetrating fraud, brings to the forefront the urgent need for ethical guidelines and regulatory frameworks to govern the use and dissemination of this technology.

Concurrently, the rise of deepfakes has catalyzed efforts to develop robust detection methods and countermeasures. The race is on to create systems capable of distinguishing between real and forged content, employing advanced machine learning techniques and forensic analysis to identify inconsistencies and anomalies in deepfake videos and images. This endeavor represents a dynamic battleground, where the forces of creation and detection are engaged in a relentless struggle, shaping the contours of a new frontier in artificial intelligence.

As we navigate through the complex narrative of image recognition, we find ourselves at a crossroads, where the awe-inspiring potential of technology meets its intricate complexities and challenges. The journey from basic facial recognition to the emergence of deepfakes illustrates the transformative power of artificial intelligence, offering a glimpse into a world where digital systems can perceive, understand, and interact with the visual world in ways that were once the realm of science fiction.

Yet, this journey also beckons us to tread carefully, fostering a landscape where technology is developed and deployed with a deep sense of responsibility and ethical consideration. As we venture further into this narrative, we are called upon to forge a path marked by innovation and integrity, crafting a future where image recognition serves as a tool for progress, enrichment, and the betterment of society.

In conclusion, the trajectory of image recognition technology, from its inception as a facial recognition tool to the emergence of deepfakes, is a vivid testament to the remarkable capabilities and inherent challenges associated with artificial intelligence. As we stand at the threshold of a new era, we are compelled to navigate this domain with a balanced approach, fostering a world where technology is harnessed for the greater good, guided by the principles of ethics, accountability, and the relentless pursuit of truth. It is a journey marked by both wonder and caution, offering a glimpse into a future where the boundaries between the real and the virtual are continually reshaped, urging us to redefine our understanding of reality in the digital age.

CHAPTER IV

Tools and Technologies

Popular programming languages for AI

In the quickly evolving landscape of artificial intelligence (AI), the role of programming languages cannot be understated. These languages serve as the backbone, the conduit that bridges human ingenuity with machine proficiency, allowing for the conceptualization and actualization of AI systems. As the demands and complexities associated with AI continue to escalate, the quest for the most competent programming languages that can adeptly navigate this dynamic field gains momentum. This section embarks on an expedition through the realms of popular programming languages that have gained prominence in artificial intelligence, highlighting their unique characteristics, advantages, and contributions to propelling the AI revolution.

In the early years of computing, programming languages like FORTRAN and Lisp marked the beginning of the journey, with the latter gaining considerable recognition as a preferred language for artificial intelligence. Developed in the late 1950s, Lisp (short for List Processing) was distinguished by its excellent support for symbolic reasoning and strong support for iterative design, both of which are intrinsic to the development of AI systems. As the wheels of time turned, more languages emerged on the horizon, each bringing something unique to the table, catalyzing the continuous growth and evolution of AI technologies.

In contemporary times, Python has emerged as a juggernaut in the sphere of artificial intelligence. Its ascent to prominence is attributed to its simple syntax, versatility, and a rich ecosystem of libraries and frameworks that are instrumental in AI development. Libraries such as TensorFlow and PyTorch have positioned Python as a darling of both novice and seasoned developers alike. The language facilitates rapid development and testing of complex algorithms and offers an unparalleled array of tools and libraries that cater to different facets of AI, including machine learning, deep learning, and natural language processing. Its inherent readability and ease of learning allow for a smoother transition from concept to implementation, a feature that has made it a staple in AI research and development environments globally.

Although initially not envisaged for such advanced computational tasks, JavaScript has also found its footing in the AI space, especially with the advent of Node.js, which allows it to be used on the server side. This universal language now supports various AI libraries and frameworks, offering the ability to integrate AI functionalities directly into web applications. Its wide usage across the web makes it a significant player, enabling the seamless integration of AI features into many web-based platforms and applications.

Java, another stalwart in the programming community, also holds a significant place in the development of AI applications. With its platform-independent characteristics, robust architecture, and strong memory management capabilities, Java offers a stable and efficient environment for building large-scale AI applications. Its object-oriented nature facilitates the encapsulation of complex algorithms into manageable code structures, aiding in developing sophisticated AI systems. Furthermore, Java's extensive community support provides a reservoir of knowledge and resources, fostering a nurturing environment for AI development.

In this vast tapestry of programming languages, we must also acknowledge the role of R, particularly in the realms of data analysis and statistical computing, which are fundamental aspects of artificial intelligence. With a rich package ecosystem, R provides a comprehensive suite of tools for data manipulation, analysis, and visualization. In the AI landscape, where data is the lifeblood fueling the development of intelligent systems, R serves as a potent tool, enabling the extraction of insightful information from vast pools of data, which aids in creating more intelligent and nuanced AI applications.

Another notable entrant in this sphere is Julia, a high-level, and high-performance programming language for technical computing. Julia combines the ease of use and flexibility of Python with the speed of C++, making it an attractive option for AI development, particularly in scenarios where computational performance is a critical factor. Its capacity to easily integrate with other programming languages and its prowess in handling mathematical and statistical computations make it a burgeoning favorite in the AI community, especially in machine learning and data science.

As we delve deeper into this narrative, we cannot overlook the contributions of languages like C++ and Perl, each having carved out a niche in the AI ecosystem. C++, with its low-level memory manipulation and high-speed computation capabilities, is often favored in scenarios where performance is a paramount consideration. On the other hand, Perl, though not a traditional choice for AI, has seen usage in various AI-related tasks owing to its strong text processing abilities, which are particularly beneficial in natural language processing tasks.

In this dynamic and ever-changing landscape, selecting an appropriate programming language is not merely a technical decision, but a strategic one, influenced by a myriad of factors including the nature of the AI project, performance requirements, and the organization's specific needs. Developers and organizations navigate this complex terrain with a clear vision and understanding, harnessing the strengths of different languages to craft AI systems that are both robust and intelligent.

In conclusion, the odyssey through the popular programming languages for artificial intelligence paints a vibrant picture of a field marked by diversity, innovation, and continuous evolution. From the early days of Lisp to the modern prominence of Python, and the growing influence of languages like Julia, we witness a rich tapestry of tools that have facilitated the growth and proliferation of AI technologies across various sectors and industries. These languages stand as the pillars supporting the edifice of artificial intelligence, providing the necessary tools and environments to foster the development of intelligent systems that can revolutionize the world as we know it. As we stand on the cusp of a new era marked by AI-driven innovations, these programming languages will be pivotal, guiding us through the next chapter of this exciting and transformative journey.

TensorFlow, PyTorch, and other AI frameworks

In the sphere of artificial intelligence, the momentum of progress is propelled not only by conceptual advancements but also by the instrumental role of frameworks that serve as the bedrock for developing sophisticated AI systems. These frameworks, equipped with many tools and functionalities, facilitate the seamless translation of theoretical concepts into practical solutions. In this context, TensorFlow and PyTorch emerge as pre-eminent figures, steering the helm of AI development, accompanied by a host of other frameworks, each contributing significantly to the multidimensional narrative of artificial intelligence. This section endeavors to unravel the intricate tapestry woven around TensorFlow, PyTorch, and other notable AI frameworks, elucidating their inherent characteristics, their symbiotic relationship with the AI community, and their indelible imprint on the trajectory of artificial intelligence.

In the vibrant ecosystem of AI frameworks, TensorFlow, developed by Google Brain, commands a significant presence. TensorFlow's emergence has been nothing short of a watershed moment in AI, ushering in a period of innovation and experimentation. Its flexible architecture allows for easy computation deployment across various platforms, be it CPUs, GPUs, or even TPUs, thus offering a versatile solution for a myriad of computational tasks. TensorFlow thrives in its capacity to facilitate deep learning and machine learning, offering a comprehensive toolkit that enables developers to craft, train, and deploy intricate neural network architectures. Its versatility is further bolstered by a high-level API, Keras, which simplifies the process of building and training models, thereby democratizing the field of AI and making it accessible to a broader audience.

Complementing TensorFlow in this dynamic landscape is PyTorch, a brainchild of Facebook's AI Research lab. With its dynamic computation graph, PyTorch offers a flexible and interactive platform for building deep learning models. This dynamism, which contrasts with TensorFlow's static computation graph, encourages a more intuitive and exploratory approach to model building, where computations can be modified on the fly, thereby offering a more pythonic and user-friendly interface. PyTorch's stronghold lies in its affinity with the research community, fostering an environment of innovation and experimentation. Its seamless integration with popular Python libraries and its ability to facilitate rapid prototyping have made it a favorite among researchers, who find its dynamic nature conducive to the experimental and iterative research and development process.

As we venture further into AI frameworks, we encounter a spectrum of other platforms, each carving out a niche in the vibrant tapestry of artificial intelligence. One such entity is Caffe, an open-source framework focusing on modularity and speed. Developed by the Berkeley Vision and Learning Center, Caffe finds particular favor in the domains of image classification and convolutional neural networks. Its modularity allows for the facile construction and manipulation of neural networks, while its emphasis on performance makes it a viable choice for large-scale industrial applications in the visual recognition space.

Adding to the rich canvas of AI frameworks is Theano, an open-source project that has served as a foundational stone in developing deep learning frameworks. Theano, with its ability to optimize and evaluate mathematical expressions, especially matrix-valued ones, set the stage for the computation on multi-dimensional arrays. Despite its discontinuation, Theano's legacy lives on, its contributions reverberating in the deep learning community and serving as a building block for modern frameworks.

In the realm of artificial intelligence, where data manipulation and analysis stand central, Apache Mahout offers a platform focused on building scalable machine learning libraries. With its ability to operate on top of Hadoop, Mahout facilitates the processing of large data sets, employing MapReduce to perform distributed computations. It offers a suite of algorithms and a framework that supports the creation of machine learning applications, particularly in collaborative filtering, clustering, and classification.

Moreover, the Microsoft Cognitive Toolkit (CNTK) stands as a testament to Microsoft's commitment to advancing the field of artificial intelligence. CNTK, with its emphasis on performance and scalability, offers a robust platform for the development of deep learning applications. Its ability to handle multiple data formats and its support for multi-machine multi-GPU backends make it a powerful tool in developing commercial-grade AI applications.

As we traverse this intricate narrative of AI frameworks, we also encounter scikit-learn, a library that has endeared itself to the data science community. Though not a framework in the traditional sense, scikit-learn's contribution to the AI space cannot be overlooked. Its focus on data mining and data analysis and its provision of a selection of simple and efficient tools for machine learning make it a vital part of the AI ecosystem.

As we come full circle in this journey through the vibrant landscape of AI frameworks, we are met with a panorama of innovation and progression. These frameworks, each with its distinctive characteristics and strengths, serve as the pillars upon which the edifice of artificial intelligence stands. They facilitate the development of intelligent systems and foster a collaborative and dynamic environment where knowledge is shared and advancements are collectively pursued. They are the crucibles where theories meet practice, where ideas are molded into tangible solutions, contributing profoundly to the evolving narrative of artificial intelligence.

In conclusion, TensorFlow, PyTorch, and the array of other AI frameworks stand as luminous beacons in artificial intelligence. They are the harbingers of a new era, an era marked by intelligent machines capable of transforming the fabric of society. From automating mundane tasks to solving complex problems, these frameworks are the driving forces propelling us into a future where the boundaries between machines and humans blur, giving rise to a symbiotic relationship marked by collaboration and mutual growth. As we stand at this intersection of time, witnessing the relentless march of artificial intelligence, these frameworks serve as our companions, guiding us through the intricate maze of AI, offering insights, tools, and the promise of a future where the potential of artificial intelligence is fully realized, ushering in a period of unprecedented growth and innovation.

Cloud AI: Services from AWS, Google, Microsoft, and others

In the contemporary technology landscape, cloud computing has emerged as a pivotal element, ushering enterprises and researchers into a new era marked by flexibility, scalability, and efficiency. Within this paradigm, Cloud AI is a prominent milestone, epitomizing the confluence of artificial intelligence with cloud computing. Technology giants such as AWS (Amazon Web Services), Google Cloud, and Microsoft Azure are leading this wave of innovation, and a cadre of other service providers, are driving the momentum of Cloud AI into uncharted territories. This section explores the expansive horizon of Cloud AI services, illuminating the offerings and contributions of these key players and others, underscoring the transformative potential of Cloud AI in reshaping the technological narrative of the modern world.

Initiating this discourse with AWS, a subsidiary of Amazon, we find a forerunner in the cloud computing domain. AWS's prowess in providing a comprehensive suite of Cloud AI services is unparalleled. With a portfolio encompassing a broad spectrum of AI functionalities, AWS has fostered an ecosystem where developers, irrespective of their expertise level, can harness the power of AI. Services such as AWS SageMaker offer an integrated environment to facilitate the building, training, and deployment of machine learning models at scale. SageMaker's appeal lies in its ability to abstract the complexities associated with machine learning, thereby allowing developers to focus on conceptualizing and implementing solutions. Further, with offerings like Rekognition for image and video analysis, Comprehend for natural language processing, and Polly for turning text into lifelike speech, AWS has curated a rich tapestry of Cloud AI services that cater to diverse industry needs, ranging from healthcare to finance, and beyond.

In tandem with AWS, Google Cloud stands as a formidable force in the Cloud AI landscape. Bringing Google's formidable expertise in artificial intelligence to the table, Google Cloud offers a series of robust AI services characterized by innovation and sophistication. With its renowned AutoML, Google Cloud has democratized the field of machine learning, offering automated solutions that enable developers to build models with minimal prior expertise. Furthermore, Google Cloud's Vision AI and Video AI provide solutions that can comprehend a vast array of visual content, facilitating applications in domains such as security and entertainment. Beyond this, its Natural Language Processing and Translation services embody the epitome of linguistic understanding and conversion, fostering a world where language barriers are obliterated, and seamless communication is facilitated. Thus, Google Cloud stands as a beacon of innovation, pioneering the integration of artificial intelligence with cloud technologies, marking a trajectory characterized by relentless advancement and exploration.

Microsoft Azure, another titan in the cloud computing arena, offers a nuanced approach to Cloud AI. Microsoft, with its rich legacy in the tech industry, leverages its expertise to craft solutions that are both cutting-edge and user-friendly. Azure AI, Microsoft's suite of AI services, encapsulates a range of functionalities designed to cater to diverse industry requirements. From Azure Machine Learning, a service that empowers developers to build, deploy, as well as manage machine learning models, to Azure Cognitive Services, which offer APIs for vision, speech, language, decision, and web search, Microsoft Azure has curated a platform that embodies versatility and innovation. Its emphasis on integrating AI with business applications, as evidenced by services like Azure Bot Service and Azure Databricks, underscores Microsoft's vision of fostering a symbiotic relationship between artificial intelligence and enterprise solutions, paving the way for a new generation of intelligent business applications that are both adaptive and intuitive.

While AWS, Google Cloud, and Microsoft Azure dominate the landscape, the narrative of Cloud AI is enriched by the contributions of other service providers who bring unique perspectives and offerings to the table. With its Watson AI, IBM Cloud offers services encompassing a wide array of functionalities, including data analytics, machine learning, and natural language processing. Oracle Cloud, another significant player, emphasizes the integration of AI with business applications, offering solutions that facilitate intelligent business processes characterized by efficiency and automation. Alibaba Cloud, a prominent entity in the Asian market, provides a comprehensive suite of AI services encompassing machine learning, deep learning, and data analytics, fostering an ecosystem of innovation and growth.

As we traverse this narrative of Cloud AI, we are met with a panorama characterized by diversity, collaboration, and relentless pursuit of innovation. These services, with their expansive and nuanced offerings, serve as conduits that facilitate the integration of artificial intelligence into the fabric of society. From automating mundane tasks to facilitating complex computations, Cloud AI services are reshaping the contours of the technological landscape, fostering an era marked by intelligence, adaptability, and efficiency.

In conclusion, the advent of Cloud AI marks a seminal moment in the annals of technology, ushering in a period characterized by unprecedented growth and transformation. As AWS, Google Cloud, Microsoft Azure, and other service providers forge ahead, carving pathways into uncharted territories, we find ourselves at the cusp of a new era, an era where the boundaries of what is possible are continually expanding, giving rise to a landscape marked by innovation, collaboration, and transformation. As we stand at this juncture, witnessing the confluence of artificial intelligence with cloud computing, we are reminded of the transformative potential of technology and its capacity to reshape industries, redefine norms, and foster an intelligent and connected world. Thus, as we navigate the expansive horizons of Cloud AI, we do so with a sense of anticipation and wonder, eager to witness the unfolding of a narrative that promises to redefine the paradigms of technology and society, steering us into a future marked by unlimited potential and possibilities.

CHAPTER V

Modern Applications of AI

Healthcare: Disease prediction, drug discovery

The healthcare sector has emerged as a focal point of innovation and transformation in recent years, significantly spurred by integrating artificial intelligence (AI) in various processes and operations. This profound intersection of healthcare and technology promises a paradigm shift that has the potential to redefine healthcare delivery and patient care. Specifically, the applications of AI in disease prediction and drug discovery are striking examples of how AI can be harnessed to foster innovation, accelerate processes, and enhance outcomes in healthcare. Through a nuanced exploration of these aspects, this section seeks to illuminate the transformative potential of AI in modern healthcare, fostering a new era marked by efficiency, accuracy, and personalized care.

Disease prediction, a critical aspect of preventive healthcare, has observed a remarkable transformation with the advent of AI. Traditional disease prediction methods, often based on a static set of variables and a linear approach, have been found wanting in terms of accuracy and predictive power. With its inherent capacity to analyze vast and complex datasets, AI has emerged as a beacon of innovation in this realm. Leveraging machine learning algorithms, AI systems can analyze patterns and trends within large datasets, encompassing variables such as genetics, lifestyle factors, and environmental influences. This holistic approach enables the creation of predictive models that are both dynamic and nuanced, allowing for more accurate predictions of disease onset and progression.

Furthermore, AI-based disease prediction models can leverage real-time data to refine and enhance their predictive capabilities continually. For instance, wearable technology and Internet of Things (IoT) devices can provide a constant stream of health data, including vital signs and biomarker levels, which can be analyzed to monitor an individual's health status and predict potential issues before they escalate. This proactive approach to disease prediction not only enhances the accuracy of predictions but also fosters a healthcare model that is preventive rather than reactive, potentially reducing the burden on healthcare systems and improving patient outcomes.

A subset of machine learning, deep learning, has also revolutionized disease prediction. Through the analysis of complex patterns within data, deep learning models can identify subtle indicators of disease that traditional methods may overlook. For example, in the field of radiology, AI algorithms have demonstrated the ability to analyze medical imaging data with a level of accuracy comparable to, and/or even surpassing, that of human experts.

These algorithms can identify patterns within imaging data indicative of conditions such as cancer, cardiovascular disease, and neurological disorders, enabling early intervention and potentially improving patient prognoses.

Parallelly, the realm of drug discovery has been profoundly impacted by the integration of AI technologies. Traditionally, the drug discovery process has been a labor-intensive and time-consuming venture, characterized by high costs and low success rates. AI can potentially disrupt this paradigm, offering tools and techniques to streamline the drug discovery process, reducing time and costs.

At the forefront of this transformation is AI's application in identifying potential drug candidates. By analyzing vast datasets encompassing molecular structures, biological pathways, and disease mechanisms, AI algorithms can identify potential drug targets and candidates with a level of speed and accuracy that is unattainable through traditional methods. Moreover, AI can facilitate the optimization of drug formulations, leveraging data analytics to identify the most effective and safe combinations of drug components.

AI has also fostered innovation in drug testing, with the development of in-silico trials that utilize computational models to replicate the effects of drugs on biological systems. These virtual trials offer a rapid, cost-effective, and ethical alternative to traditional animal and human trials, potentially accelerating the drug development process and bringing effective therapies to market more quickly.

Furthermore, using AI in clinical trials can enhance the efficiency and effectiveness of these critical phases of drug development. AI can facilitate the identification of suitable participants for clinical trials, analyze real-time data to monitor trial progress, and identify potential issues before they escalate, thereby reducing the risk of trial failures and making sure the safety and well-being of participants.

As we venture deeper into the realms of AI-enabled healthcare, we witness a convergence of technology and medicine that holds unprecedented potential. Integrating AI in disease prediction fosters a proactive approach to healthcare, where diseases can be predicted and prevented before they manifest, promoting a society marked by health and wellness. Simultaneously, the incorporation of AI in drug discovery heralds a new era of innovation as well as efficiency, where effective therapies can be developed more rapidly and at a lower cost, potentially revolutionizing the treatment of many diseases.

In conclusion, the modern applications of AI in healthcare, particularly in the domains of disease prediction and drug discovery, represent a transformative force that has the potential to redefine the healthcare landscape. By harnessing AI's analytical prowess and predictive capabilities, we stand on the brink of a healthcare revolution characterized by personalized care, improved outcomes, and enhanced efficiency. As we navigate this transformative journey, we do so with a sense of anticipation and hope, eager to witness the unfolding of a new chapter in healthcare, a chapter marked by innovation, collaboration, and the relentless pursuit of excellence, steering us toward a future where healthcare delivery is not only efficient and effective, but also compassionate and personalized, fostering a world marked by health, wellbeing, and prosperity for all.

Automotive: Self-driving cars

In the evolution of transportation, the advent of automobiles marked a seminal point, revolutionizing mobility and ushering societies into new eras of development and connectivity. Today, we find ourselves at the cusp of yet another radical transformation within the automotive sector – integrating artificial intelligence (AI) in the genesis of self-driving or autonomous vehicles. The confluence of technology and mobility is redefining the contours of the automotive industry and promises to reshape urban landscapes, redefine transportation norms, and foster a new epoch of safety, efficiency, and environmental sustainability. This section seeks to delve into the rich tapestry of modern applications of AI in the automotive sector, with a particular focus on the revolutionary development of self-driving cars, exploring their mechanics, implications, and the future they herald.

At the heart of the autonomous vehicle movement is the intricate integration of various AI technologies that work synergistically to create a vehicle capable of navigating the complexities of modern roads with minimal or no human intervention. These technologies encompass many components, including but not limited to, machine learning algorithms, deep neural networks, computer vision, and sensor fusion technologies. Together, these create a cohesive system capable of perceiving, interpreting, and reacting to the dynamic environment of the road.

Machine learning and deep neural networks form the crux of AI integration, empowering the vehicle to process and analyze data from various sensors and input sources in real time. These technologies enable the vehicle to learn and adapt to different driving conditions, traffic patterns, and potential hazards, fostering a continually evolving system and improving performance. This learning process is facilitated through the collection and analysis of vast datasets, which encompass numerous driving scenarios and conditions, allowing the vehicle to develop a nuanced understanding of driving dynamics.

In parallel, computer vision and sensor fusion technologies are pivotal in enabling the autonomous vehicle to perceive and interpret its surroundings. Advanced sensors, including LIDAR (Light Detection and Ranging), radar, and cameras, are integrated into the vehicle, providing a comprehensive view of the environment. These sensors can detect objects, vehicles, pedestrians, and other elements with high precision, forming the basis of the vehicle's perception system. Computer vision algorithms then analyze this data, facilitating object recognition, tracking, and trajectory prediction, thereby enabling the vehicle to navigate its surroundings safely and efficiently.

Another critical aspect of autonomous vehicles is the development of advanced control systems that can seamlessly integrate the outputs from the perception and decision-making modules to execute safe and smooth driving maneuvers. These control systems are designed to be adaptive and adjust to varying road conditions and driving scenarios, ensuring optimal vehicle performance and safety. Furthermore, Vehicle-to-Everything (V2X) communication technologies are being integrated into autonomous vehicles, fostering communication between vehicles and infrastructure, enhancing situational awareness and further augmenting safety.

As we delve deeper into the implications of this transformative technology, we encounter a series of potential benefits that hold the promise of revolutionizing transportation. Firstly, the advent of autonomous vehicles heralds the potential for significant improvements in road safety. By eliminating human error, which is a primary cause of road accidents, autonomous vehicles can potentially reduce the incidence of collisions, saving lives and reducing injuries. Moreover, integrating advanced sensors and AI algorithms allows these vehicles to react more quickly and accurately to potential hazards, further enhancing safety.

Furthermore, autonomous vehicles have the potential to revolutionize urban transportation, fostering more efficient and sustainable mobility solutions. By integrating intelligent transportation systems and smart city infrastructure, autonomous vehicles can facilitate optimized traffic flow, reducing congestion and enhancing the efficiency of urban transportation networks. Moreover, these vehicles promise to reduce environmental impacts, as they can be integrated with electric propulsion systems, reducing emissions and fostering a cleaner, greener urban environment.

Moreover, the rise of autonomous vehicles opens up new vistas of opportunity within the automotive industry, fostering innovation and generating new business models. The traditional vehicle ownership and usage paradigms are being challenged, giving rise to new mobility solutions, including autonomous ride-sharing and ride-hailing services, which can offer more accessible and affordable transportation options. Furthermore, the automotive industry is witnessing a convergence with the tech industry, as collaborations and partnerships between automotive manufacturers and tech companies are fostering rapid innovation and development within the autonomous vehicle sector.

However, the journey towards fully autonomous mobility is challenging. Issues about regulatory frameworks, ethical considerations, and cybersecurity are significant hurdles that need to be addressed. Developing comprehensive regulatory guidelines that govern the testing and deployment of autonomous vehicles is critical, ensuring that these vehicles meet stringent safety and performance standards. Moreover, ethical considerations, particularly in the context of decision-making algorithms in critical situations, need to be carefully evaluated, fostering a system that is not only technologically advanced but also ethically sound. Furthermore, securing these complex systems against potential cyber-attacks is of paramount importance, ensuring the safety and security of users and the broader transportation ecosystem.

In conclusion, the integration of AI in the automotive sector, epitomized by the development of autonomous vehicles, represents a transformative force that has the potential to redefine the paradigms of mobility and transportation. As we stand at the cusp of this new era, we find ourselves amidst a narrative that is characterized by innovation, collaboration, and the relentless pursuit of a safer, more efficient, and sustainable mobility future. Both opportunities and challenges mark the journey towards autonomous mobility, as societies navigate the complexities of integrating these advanced systems into the fabric of urban landscapes. As we venture forth, it is with a sense of anticipation and hope, eager to witness the unfolding of a new chapter in the annals of transportation, a chapter that promises to steer us into a future marked by safety, efficiency, and environmental sustainability, fostering a world that is not only connected but also intelligent and responsive to the evolving requirements and aspirations of societies.

Finance: Algorithmic trading, credit risk modelling

The finance sector has witnessed a paradigm shift in the last few decades, spearheaded by computing technology advancements and data proliferation. Among the various transformations, the rise of artificial intelligence (AI) and machine learning (ML) has emerged as a significant disruptor, fundamentally altering the landscape of financial processes and systems. Mainly, algorithmic trading and credit risk modeling are two realms where the influence of AI is profoundly felt, driving innovation, efficiency, and accuracy. This section aims to elucidate the transformative impacts of AI in these domains, illustrating the nuanced intricacies and the future trajectory of finance in the age of artificial intelligence.

Algorithmic trading, often called algo-trading or high-frequency trading, represents the nexus where finance meets cutting-edge technology. It entails using complex AI algorithms to execute trades at a speed and frequency that is humanly impossible. Through this approach, trading firms can analyze many financial instruments in real time, evaluating market conditions from various data sources to execute trades with pinpoint accuracy and timing.

At its core, algorithmic trading leverages mathematical models and computational algorithms to analyze market data and identify trading opportunities. These opportunities might be based on various factors such as price, volume, and order book dynamics. The central premise is to capitalize on market inefficiencies and fluctuations, with algorithms that can react to market changes in fractions of a second. Not only does this approach enable rapid execution of trades, but it also minimizes human error, a factor that historically has been responsible for significant losses in the financial markets.

Furthermore, AI and machine learning are adding new dimensions to algorithmic trading, facilitating the development of predictive models that can analyze vast arrays of data points to determine patterns and trends that might be elusive to human traders. These models can incorporate traditional financial metrics and alternative data sources like social media sentiment, news feeds, and economic indicators, providing a more holistic view of the market dynamics.

This ability to process and analyze big data in real time allows for more sophisticated and nuanced trading strategies, potentially leading to higher profitability.

Moreover, AI-based trading systems are capable of self-learning, meaning that they can adapt and evolve in response to changing market conditions. This attribute is a stark departure from traditional trading systems, which might be rigid and unable to adapt quickly to market shifts. Through machine learning, trading algorithms can continually refine their strategies, improving their predictive accuracy and maximizing potential profits.

However, the rise of algorithmic trading also brings forth a set of challenges and concerns. Firstly, the increased speed and complexity of trades can lead to heightened volatility and systemic risks. Flash crashes, wherein markets experience sudden and extreme price swings, have been attributed to algorithmic trading. Furthermore, the reliance on AI and technology raises cybersecurity concerns, with trading platforms potentially being targets for hacking and manipulation. Additionally, the ethical implications of AI-driven trading, which might exacerbate market inequalities and create barriers for retail investors, are subjects of ongoing debate.

Parallel to the innovations in trading, the financial sector is witnessing a revolution in credit risk modeling, a critical aspect of financial risk management. Traditionally, credit risk modeling has relied on a set of static parameters, including credit history, financial statements, and other relevant metrics. However, with the occurence of AI and machine learning, the domain is experiencing a radical transformation.

AI facilitates a more dynamic and comprehensive approach to credit risk modeling. By integrating machine learning algorithms, financial institutions can analyze a much wider array of data points to assess credit risk more accurately. This might include unconventional data sources such as online behavior, social media activity, and even geolocation data, providing a more granular view of a borrower's creditworthiness.

Moreover, AI enables real-time monitoring and analysis, allowing financial institutions to identify potential risks and red flags promptly. Predictive analytics, powered by machine learning, can potentially forecast default probabilities with greater accuracy, enabling financial institutions to mitigate risks proactively. In addition to reducing losses, this proactive strategy for risk management strengthens the financial system.

Furthermore, AI facilitates the development of automated underwriting systems, which can streamline the credit assessment process, reducing the time and resources required to evaluate credit applications. This efficiency potentially translates to lower costs and increased accessibility for borrowers, fostering financial inclusion and democratizing access to financial services.

However, similar to algorithmic trading, the integration of AI in credit risk modeling presents challenges. Using non-traditional data sources raises privacy and ethical concerns, with potential biases in

AI algorithms being a significant issue. Ensuring the fairness and transparency of AI-driven credit risk models is a critical consideration, necessitating regulatory oversight and ethical guidelines.

In conclusion, the fusion of artificial intelligence with finance, particularly in the realms of algorithmic trading and credit risk modeling, is fostering a new era of innovation and efficiency. The ability to analyze vast datasets in real time, identify nuanced patterns, and react swiftly to market dynamics stands as a testament to the transformative potential of AI. However, this journey is not devoid of challenges, with increased volatility, systemic risks, and ethical considerations being significant hurdles. As the financial sector navigates this transformative journey, a balanced approach that leverages the advantages of AI while mitigating its potential downsides will be critical. In the age of artificial intelligence, the future of finance promises to be dynamic, nuanced, and profoundly transformative, heralding a new epoch of innovation, efficiency, and inclusivity.

Entertainment: Content recommendation, virtual characters

The entertainment industry, a burgeoning force of creativity and innovation, has always been at the forefront of adopting novel technologies to enhance audiences' experience worldwide. Artificial intelligence (AI), a field that has shown unprecedented growth and development in recent years, has significantly permeated the entertainment sector, fundamentally transforming the landscape and offering a dynamic array of possibilities. The integration of AI in content recommendation systems and the creation of virtual characters stand as two prominent manifestations of this synergy, reflecting a convergence of art and technology that is reshaping the contours of entertainment in the contemporary era. This section delves deep into these aspects, elucidating the complexity and the ingenuity that AI brings to the world of entertainment.

The genesis of AI's profound impact in the entertainment sphere can be prominently observed in content recommendation systems employed by various digital platforms. These systems, adept at analyzing and understanding intricate user preferences patterns, have revolutionized how content is consumed and distributed. In an era where the volume of content is immensely vast, the role of intelligent recommendation systems has become pivotal, guiding users through a labyrinth of choices to discover content that resonates with their preferences and tastes.

At the heart of these recommendation systems lies sophisticated algorithms capable of sifting through a deluge of data to identify patterns and correlations. These algorithms scrutinize various parameters such as viewing histories, user ratings, and demographic information to create a nuanced understanding of user preferences. Furthermore, advancements in machine learning and deep learning have endowed these systems with the ability to learn and evolve with time, continually refining their accuracy and predictive capabilities. As a result, users are presented with a curated selection of content, which aligns with their tastes and potentially broadens their horizons by introducing them to new genres and styles.

However, this marriage of technology and entertainment is not without its set of challenges. While enhancing user experience, the personalized approach has also given rise to concerns regarding data privacy and the potential for manipulation. Furthermore, the echo chamber effect, a phenomenon where users are exclusively exposed to content and opinions similar to their own, is a notable downside, potentially limiting the diversity of content users encounter. As these systems evolve, striking a balance between personalization and diversity will be crucial, fostering an ecosystem that respects user autonomy while encouraging a rich and varied entertainment experience.

Parallel to the development of content recommendation systems, the realm of virtual characters represents another fascinating frontier where AI is making significant strides. Virtual characters, often embedded in video games, movies, and virtual reality experiences, stand as a testament to the seamless blend of creativity and technology, offering immersive and interactive experiences that were once confined to the realm of science fiction.

With the aid of AI, virtual characters are no longer static entities confined to scripted behaviors. Instead, they have evolved into dynamic beings capable of exhibiting a range of emotions, reactions, and actions that mirror the complexity of human behavior. Machine learning algorithms, neural networks, and also natural language processing techniques have been instrumental in this evolution, facilitating the creation of characters that can understand as well as respond to user inputs naturally and believably.

These characters, equipped with a deep understanding of human psychology and behavior, can adapt and respond to users in real time, offering unprecedented interaction and immersion. Furthermore, AI has facilitated the development of virtual influencers and artists, digital entities that interact with audiences on social media platforms, offering a new dimension of celebrity culture and entertainment. With their unique personas and narratives, these virtual beings are reshaping the boundaries of storytelling and entertainment, offering glimpses into a future where the line between the virtual and the real is increasingly blurred.

Furthermore, the world of animation and filmmaking has also witnessed a renaissance through the integration of AI. Advanced algorithms can automate various aspects of the production process, including scripting, animation, and editing, drastically reducing the time and resources required to create high-quality content. Moreover, AI has facilitated the creation of deepfakes, a technology that allows for manipulating video and audio content to create hyper-realistic, yet fabricated, media. While this technology offers exciting possibilities for content creation, it also poses significant ethical and moral challenges, necessitating vigilant oversight and regulation.

As we navigate through this era of convergence, it is evident that artificial intelligence is poised to redefine the contours of the entertainment industry. Through intelligent content recommendation systems and the creation of dynamic virtual characters, AI offers a landscape of possibilities, fostering innovation and enhancing the richness of the entertainment experience. However, this journey is accompanied by a set of challenges and dilemmas, reflecting the complexities of integrating advanced technology into the intricate fabric of human culture and expression.

In conclusion, integrating artificial intelligence in the entertainment sector represents a dynamic and evolving frontier in which technology meets creativity to forge new paradigms and experiences. The developments in content recommendation and virtual characters signify a shift towards a more personalized and immersive form of entertainment, a trend that is likely to continue in the coming years. As we stand at the cusp of this transformation, it is essential to navigate this terrain with a sense of caution and responsibility, fostering a landscape that respects the nuances of human experience while leveraging the potential of artificial intelligence to create a richer, more diverse, and engaging entertainment ecosystem for generations to come. The future of entertainment, under the aegis of AI, promises to be a vibrant and exciting journey, offering glimpses into new realms of creativity and innovation that redefine the boundaries of what is possible in the entertainment world.

CHAPTER VI

Ethical Implications

The potential biases in AI and the dangers of unchecked algorithms

In recent years, the ascendancy of artificial intelligence (AI) has reshaped various aspects of contemporary society, carving a trajectory of unprecedented advancement and innovation. Yet, as these developments permeate diverse sectors ranging from healthcare to finance, they simultaneously unveil intrinsic flaws — biases encoded in algorithms, and the potential dangers that lurk when these algorithms operate unchecked. This section seeks to delve deep into this critical facet of AI, elucidating the potential biases inherent in the AI systems and the perils that arise from unchecked algorithms, thereby highlighting the need for a reasonable approach towards deploying these technologies.

At the core of the discussion on AI biases is the understanding that these systems learn and adapt depending on the data they are fed. It is an unfortunate yet irrefutable fact that these data pools often carry the imprints of societal biases, prejudices, and disparities that have persisted over centuries. Whether it is racial prejudice, gender discrimination, or socioeconomic disparities, the data used to train AI systems often encapsulates these biases, inadvertently weaving them into the very fabric of AI algorithms. Consequently, instead of mitigating societal prejudices, AI systems can sometimes amplify them, giving rise to a cycle of reinforcement that further entrenches these biases in society.

Consider the recruitment domain, where AI-driven tools are increasingly utilized to sift through a deluge of applications to identify suitable candidates. When historical data indicates a preference for candidates from specific demographics, an unchecked algorithm would perpetuate this trend, sidelining potentially deserving candidates who do not conform to these patterns. This kind of systemic bias undermines the principles of equality and fairness and deprives organizations of a diverse and vibrant workforce known to foster innovation and productivity.

Similarly, in law enforcement, the deployment of AI tools for predictive policing has come under scrutiny for potentially exacerbating existing biases. These systems, which utilize historical data to predict areas of potential criminal activity, may inadvertently focus disproportionately on communities that have been over-policed in the past, perpetuating a cycle of surveillance and mistrust. These instances underscore the criticality of scrutinizing the data and the algorithms that power AI systems to ensure they do not become conduits for perpetuating societal biases and disparities.

Yet, the ramifications of unchecked algorithms extend beyond the reinforcement of existing biases. In some cases, they can give rise to new forms of discrimination and exclusion, creating nuanced challenges that are complex to unravel. For instance, AI systems in the financial sector, tasked with assessing the creditworthiness of individuals, might rely on a myriad of factors including spending habits and social connections, potentially leading to unjustified exclusions or discriminatory practices.

Moreover, the opacity of AI algorithms, often described as "black boxes," exacerbates these challenges. The complexity of these systems and a lack of transparency can make it difficult to pinpoint the origins of biases and implement corrective measures. This opacity also creates a barrier to accountability, making it challenging to ascertain responsibility when things go awry.

Furthermore, unchecked algorithms can potentially manipulate individuals and society at large. In the domain of social media, AI-driven algorithms designed to maximize user engagement have been criticized for fostering polarization and misinformation. By prioritizing content eliciting strong reactions, these algorithms can create echo chambers, where individuals are exposed predominantly to information and opinions that align with their beliefs. This can fuel polarization, undermine democratic discourse, and potentially give rise to radicalization.

As we navigate this complex terrain, it becomes apparent that addressing unchecked algorithms' potential biases and dangers is not merely a technical challenge but a deeply ethical one. It necessitates a multidisciplinary approach encompassing technological advancements and insights from sociology, psychology, and ethics. Implementing safeguards against biases, fostering transparency, and ensuring accountability should be paramount considerations in developing and deploying AI systems.

The evolving discourse on the ethical dimensions of AI has sparked a call for the development of frameworks and guidelines that prioritize fairness, inclusivity, and transparency. Organizations and governments increasingly recognize the need to institute mechanisms for regularly auditing AI systems to detect and mitigate biases and foster an environment of accountability. Additionally, there is a growing prominence on incorporating ethics into the AI development process, fostering a culture of responsibility and vigilance among developers and practitioners.

In conclusion, as society stands at the cusp of an era dominated by artificial intelligence, we must navigate this journey with a deep sense of responsibility and caution. The potential biases embedded in AI systems, and the dangers of unchecked algorithms, represent pressing challenges that necessitate concerted efforts from various stakeholders - developers, policymakers, and society at large. To harness the full potential of AI, it is imperative to approach these technologies with a nuanced understanding of the intricate interplay between machines and the human society they serve.

As we forge ahead into a future intertwined with artificial intelligence, let us strive to build systems that not only epitomize the pinnacle of technological innovation but also embody the principles of justice, fairness, and inclusivity. Only through an informed and conscious approach can we ensure that the AI revolution fosters a society that is not only technologically advanced but also just and humane. The journey ahead is complex and fraught with challenges, but with vigilance and collaboration, we can aspire to build a future where artificial intelligence serves as a beacon of progress, illuminating pathways to a more equitable and harmonious world.

The job displacement debate

In the contemporary world, a narrative that has found itself at the center of numerous debates is the trajectory of job displacement owing to the rapid advancements in artificial intelligence as well as automation technologies. The emergence of machines capable of performing tasks once exclusively managed by humans has kindled fear and anticipation in equal measure, fostering discussions that span various perspectives and opinions. This section seeks to navigate the intricate and sometimes contentious corridors of the job displacement debate, unraveling the nuances and complexities that characterize this pressing issue of modern times.

At the outset, it is essential to acknowledge that the fear of technology-induced job displacement is not a novelty of the twenty-first century. Historically, technological advancements have often been viewed through a prism of apprehension, with the introduction of new machinery often met with resistance due to fears of ensuing job losses. From the Luddite movement during the Industrial Revolution to the automation scares of the 1960s, each wave of technological advancement has ignited debates about potential job displacement. However, these transition periods have also led to new job categories and the evolution of existing roles, suggesting a dynamic, if not entirely harmonious, relationship between technology and labor markets.

In the current epoch, the burgeoning capabilities of artificial intelligence stand as a testimony to human ingenuity and a potential harbinger of job displacement on a scale hitherto unseen. Machines equipped with AI can analyze vast quantities of data at unprecedented speeds, perform complex calculations, and even learn and adapt over time. These capabilities have enabled the automation of a wide array of tasks, ranging from routine and repetitive tasks in manufacturing to complex and nuanced tasks in fields such as finance and healthcare.

The proponents of the disruptive potential of AI argue that the speed and scale of current advancements pose a significant threat to the labor market. They caution that AI could outpace the ability of economies to generate new jobs, leading to widespread unemployment and social unrest. This perspective is underscored by numerous studies and forecasts that predict a considerable portion of existing jobs being at risk of automation in the coming decades.

For instance, jobs that are heavily reliant on routine tasks and predictable activities are perceived to be at higher risk. Manual labor jobs in manufacturing, transportation, and retail industries are often cited as particularly vulnerable to displacement due to automation. Moreover, the advancement in natural language processing and machine learning algorithms has also opened up the possibility of automating tasks in professions that were once considered immune to automation, including journalism, law, and medicine, thereby broadening the spectrum of potentially impacted jobs.

Conversely, a school of thought maintains a more optimistic view of the interaction between AI and job markets. This perspective suggests that adopting AI technologies will indeed lead to the displacement of specific jobs, but it will simultaneously foster the creation of new job categories and opportunities. Proponents of this view contend that AI can complement human labor, augmenting human capabilities and freeing individuals from routine and mundane tasks, thereby allowing them to concentrate on more creative and complex activities.

Furthermore, it is posited that AI has the potential to spur economic growth, fueling demand for labor in sectors that may not yet exist. The historical trajectory of technological advancements lends weight to this perspective, illustrating that innovation has often led to expanding job opportunities over time, albeit with a shift in the nature and type of jobs available.

Nevertheless, the transition is unlikely to be seamless. Even if the net impact on job numbers is neutral or positive, job displacement and creation will likely create significant challenges. Workers who find their skills obsolete may face difficulties in transitioning to new roles, necessitating substantial investments in retraining and upskilling programs. Moreover, there is a danger of increasing inequality, as the benefits of AI may accrue disproportionately to individuals with high skill levels and to firms that can harness the potential of these technologies effectively.

Furthermore, the geographical distribution of jobs may undergo a shift, with regions that are heavily dependent on industries at risk of automation potentially facing substantial economic and social disruptions. Policymakers thus find themselves at a critical juncture, tasked with navigating the complex dynamics of the AI-induced transition in the labor market.

Addressing the potential challenges of job displacement necessitates a multi-faceted approach that encompasses education policy, labor market interventions, and social safety nets. Educational institutions will need to adapt to the changing landscape, fostering the development of skills that are complementary to AI technologies. Labor market policies will need to facilitate the transition of workers from declining sectors to emerging sectors, possibly through targeted retraining programs and incentives for firms to invest in skill development.

In conclusion, the job displacement debate represents one of the AI era's most pressing and complex challenges. The potential for widespread job displacement ignites fears of social and economic disruption, fostering a narrative oscillating between pessimism and optimism. As we venture further into a world intertwined with artificial intelligence, it becomes increasingly imperative to approach this transition with a nuanced understanding, preparing for potential disruptions while also harnessing these technologies' opportunities.

A balanced approach that recognizes the potential risks while fostering innovation and adaptation will be critical in navigating the road ahead. By promoting dialogue and collaboration between various stakeholders, including governments, industries, and educational institutions, society can aspire to navigate the tumultuous waters of the AI revolution, steering towards a future where technology catalyzes progress, fostering economic growth and enhancing the quality of life for all. It is a journey fraught with challenges, but with foresight and collaboration, a harmonious symbiosis between AI and the labor market remains within the realm of possibility.

Surveillance and privacy concerns

In a world ever increasingly enmeshed in technological advancements, the realms of surveillance and privacy have intertwined to form a complex narrative that reverberates with echoes of Orwellian concerns. This narrative is characterized by the unrelenting advancement of artificial intelligence and its integration into diverse facets of human existence. The landscape is riddled with many intricacies, from personal privacy concerns to global security and surveillance dynamics debates. This section explores this labyrinthine narrative, examining the intersections of surveillance and privacy concerns that have become focal points in contemporary discourse.

At the outset, it is indispensable to delineate the landscape that has set the stage for the evolving narrative on surveillance and privacy. The inception of the internet heralded a new era, a global village interconnected in hitherto unimaginable ways. The proliferation of smart devices and also advances in artificial intelligence has exponentially expanded data collection and analysis capacities. Governments, corporations, and various organizations have harnessed these technologies to keep tabs on myriad aspects of human activity, fostering a surveillance ecosystem that is both pervasive and, at times, intrusive.

The rise of social media platforms marked a significant milestone in this trajectory, transforming interaction and information exchange modalities. Concurrently, these platforms became fertile grounds for collecting personal data, a trove of information that could be analyzed, monetized, and utilized for various purposes. The commodification of personal data has raised alarm bells, sparking debates on the boundaries of privacy and the ethical considerations that underpin the collection and use of such data.

Furthermore, governments across the globe have embraced surveillance technologies as tools for maintaining security and order. These technologies range from closed-circuit television cameras to sophisticated algorithms capable of analyzing vast swathes of data to identify potential threats. In many instances, these surveillance mechanisms have proved invaluable in combating crime, terrorism, and other forms of social malaise. However, these developments have not been without controversy. The deployment of these technologies has often been accompanied by concerns regarding the infringement of individual privacy rights, fueling debates on the delicate balance between security and privacy.

As we venture further into this discourse, it becomes apparent that the dynamics of surveillance and privacy are deeply entrenched in a web of complex ethical, legal, and social considerations. One of the central tenets of this narrative is the concept of consent. The collection and use of personal data often hinge on the consent of the individuals whose data is being harvested. However, concerns have been raised about the transparency and authenticity of the consent mechanisms employed by various entities. Critics argue that individuals are often not fully informed about the extent to which their data is being used and the potential ramifications of such usage.

Moreover, the internet's and digital technologies' global nature has fostered a landscape where data flows seamlessly across borders, further complicating the dynamics of surveillance and privacy. Different jurisdictions have varied approaches to privacy protection, creating a patchwork of legal frameworks that govern the collection and use of personal data. This fragmentation has raised challenges in ensuring comprehensive protection of individual privacy, particularly in a world where data has become a valuable commodity.

The issue of surveillance extends beyond governments and corporations to encompass societal dynamics. The generation of smart devices has facilitated the emergence of a phenomenon often called "sousveillance," wherein individuals utilize technology to surveil each other. This facet of surveillance culture further blurs the boundaries of privacy, fostering a landscape where the personal and the public become increasingly intertwined.

Furthermore, advances in artificial intelligence have facilitated the development of sophisticated surveillance technologies that can analyze and interpret data in unprecedented ways. Facial recognition technology, for instance, has become a cornerstone in surveillance systems, capable of accurately identifying individuals. However, these technologies have been met with skepticism and opposition, with critics pointing to the potential for misuse and the dangers of mass surveillance.

These technological advancements have also exacerbated concerns regarding biases and discrimination. Algorithms are often trained on data sets that may contain inherent biases, potentially perpetuating and amplifying existing prejudices and disparities. Consequently, deploying these technologies in surveillance systems has raised questions about the potential for discriminatory practices and undermining social justice and equality.

As society grapples with these pressing concerns, there is a burgeoning consensus on the need for a robust regulatory framework to safeguard individual privacy while allowing for the responsible use of surveillance technologies. Privacy advocates call for implementing principles such as data minimization, where the collection of personal data is limited to what is strictly necessary. Moreover, there is a push for greater transparency and accountability in using surveillance technologies, fostering a landscape where individuals are empowered to have greater control over their personal data.

At the crux of this discourse lies a fundamental question about the kind of society we aspire to build in the digital age. The tension between surveillance and privacy embodies a more profound struggle, a negotiation between the collective and the individual, between security and liberty. As we navigate this complex terrain, it becomes incumbent upon society to foster an inclusive and nuanced dialogue that weighs the potential benefits of surveillance technologies against the possible infringements on individual privacy

In conclusion, the narrative on surveillance and privacy in the era of artificial intelligence is characterized by a complex interplay of technological advancements, societal dynamics, and ethical considerations. The proliferation of surveillance technologies has fostered a landscape rife with concerns regarding the erosion of privacy and the potential for misuse. However, these technologies also promise to enhance security and foster a safer society.

As we stand at this critical juncture, the path forward requires a collaborative approach that brings together governments, industry stakeholders, and civil society to forge a balanced and responsible framework for deploying surveillance technologies. It necessitates a reevaluation of existing legal and ethical frameworks, fostering a landscape that respects individual privacy while also harnessing the potential of technology to enhance societal well-being.

Ultimately, the journey ahead is fraught with challenges and uncertainties. However, through concerted effort and a commitment to upholding the principles of justice, equality, as well as human dignity, society can aspire to navigate the intricate corridors of the surveillance and privacy narrative, steering toward a future that embodies the harmonious coexistence of technology and humanity. It is a delicate balancing act that calls for wisdom, foresight, and deep-seated respect for the intrinsic value of individual privacy in the fabric of a democratic and just society.

CHAPTER VII

AI in Popular Culture

Science fiction's influence: Movies, books, and their predictions

In the intricate mosaic of human culture, art has often served as a mirror reflecting society's aspirations, fears, and conjectures about the unknown future. The relationship between artificial intelligence (AI) and science fiction is a rich symbiosis where art explores the labyrinthine implications of machine intelligence, often predicting and inspiring real technological advancements. From literature to cinema, science fiction has not only foreseen the advent of AI but has also posed vital philosophical questions and offered vivid illustrations of a world harmonizing with or succumbing to artificial beings. This section will delve into this fascinating interplay, exploring how science fiction, through movies and books, has envisioned the trajectory of AI and its profound influence on society.

At the genesis of this discourse, it is pertinent to address the first waves of science fiction literature that ventured into the domain of AI. As early as the 19th century, narratives began to sprout, hinting at the concept of machines possessing intelligence. Mary Shelley's "Frankenstein" (1818) can be seen as a primordial glimpse into man's creation of life through artificial means, although not explicitly within the domain of AI. As we move forward in time, Karel Čapek introduced the world to the concept of robots in his play "R.U.R." (Rossum's Universal Robots) in 1920, portraying artificial beings created to serve humans but eventually leading to humanity's downfall, an early forewarning of the potential perils of AI.

The literary voyage into the realm of AI blossomed in the 20th century with visionary authors like Isaac Asimov, who not only imagined a future populated with intelligent robots but also laid down the fundamental laws governing their behavior, famously known as Asimov's Three Laws of Robotics. These laws, introduced in his series of stories collected under "I, Robot" (1950), have since formed the philosophical backbone of many real-world discussions concerning the ethical programming of artificial intelligence. Philip K. Dick, another stalwart in science fiction literature, ventured deep into the psychological and moral dimensions of AI in works such as "Do Androids Dream of Electric Sheep?" (1968), later adapted into the film "Blade Runner" (1982), where the lines between humans and artificial beings blur, raising poignant questions about consciousness and identity.

Parallel to the blossoming of science fiction literature, the silver screen became a vibrant canvas where filmmakers painted their visions of a world integrated with AI. Cinematic journeys into the realms of AI often oscillated between utopian dreams and dystopian nightmares. Films like "Metropolis" (1927) offered early depictions of robots, embodying fears of industrialization and the dehumanization it potentially brought. As the technology progressed, so did the complexity and realism of AI portrayals in cinema. "2001: A Space Odyssey" (1968), depending on Arthur C. Clarke's novel, presented HAL 9000, an AI with sinister undertones, embodying the fears of machines turning against their creators, a theme that would be echoed in numerous subsequent narratives.

The 1980s and 1990s witnessed a burgeoning of AI narratives in cinema, with movies like "Terminator" (1984) painting a grim picture of AI-powered machines orchestrating a rebellion against humanity. These movies entertained and served as cautionary tales, fostering discussions on the potential ramifications of unchecked advancements in AI technology. On the flip side, films like "Bicentennial Man" (1999), adapted from an Asimov story, offered a more optimistic view, portraying a robot's centuries-long journey towards acquiring humanity, hence illustrating the potential for harmony and mutual growth between humans and artificial beings.

As we entered the new millennium, the intricacies of AI narratives in science fiction became even more nuanced and sophisticated. Movies like "A.I. Artificial Intelligence" (2001) explored the emotional dimensions of artificial beings, offering viewers a deeply moving narrative that pondered on the nature of consciousness and the ethical implications of creating beings capable of emotions and desires. Moreover, films like "Her" (2013) delved into the realms of AI-human relationships, exploring the complexities of love and companionship in a world where AI can potentially embody all the attributes of a sentient, empathetic entity.

Parallel to the visual narratives, literature continued its exploration with novels like "Rainbows End" (2006) by Vernor Vinge, which envisioned a world transformed by augmented reality and artificial intelligence, offering a glimpse into the potential integration of AI into daily life and its implications on society and individual identities. With works like "Neuromancer" (1984) by William Gibson, the cyberpunk genre further enriched the tapestry of AI narratives, introducing audiences to dystopian cybernetic futures where AI forms an intrinsic part of a gritty, technology-driven landscape.

The influence of these narratives on the real-world development and perception of AI cannot be understated. Science fiction has often served as a fertile ground for scientists, technologists, and visionaries to find inspiration and cautionary tales. The vivid portrayals of AI in books and movies have fueled the imagination of many pioneers in the field, guiding and shaping the trajectory of AI research and development. Moreover, science fiction has played a pivotal role in fostering public discourse on AI, shaping perceptions, and facilitating a broader understanding of the complex issues surrounding artificial intelligence.

In conclusion, the dance between AI and science fiction is a vibrant and evolving narrative, a symbiotic relationship where art and science influence and inspire each other in a continuous cycle of imagination and innovation. Through the lens of science fiction, society has been offered glimpses into potential futures, where AI holds the promise of revolutionizing life as we know it, offering unprecedented opportunities and posing profound challenges.

Books and movies have served as both a canvas and a mirror, reflecting society's aspirations and apprehensions concerning artificial intelligence. As AI continues its march forward, becoming an ever more potent force in society, the science fiction genre will undoubtedly continue its role as a vital mediator, fostering dialogue, posing critical philosophical questions, and offering visionary glimpses into the potential pathways and pitfalls that lie ahead in the AI odyssey. Through this rich and ongoing narrative, society is provided a prism through which to explore, understand, and navigate the complex and ever-evolving landscape of artificial intelligence in a quest for a future where technology and humanity can flourish in harmony.

How pop culture shapes and reflects society's view on AI

The nuanced interplay between pop culture and the unfolding narrative of Artificial Intelligence (AI) is a prism through which society's evolving perspectives, hopes, fears, and ethical dilemmas regarding technology are reflected and shaped. Pop culture, encompassing mediums such as literature, cinema, music, and art, serves as a dynamic canvas where the intricate dance between humans and machines is vividly portrayed. This section explores the symbiotic relationship between pop culture and AI, delving into the nuances of how popular media both molds and mirrors society's stance on this groundbreaking technology.

At the heart of pop culture's portrayal of AI lies a complex mosaic of narratives that intertwine anticipation with apprehension. Over the decades, the lens of pop culture has magnified both the fascinating prospects and the foreboding implications of a future intertwined with machine intelligence. As AI technology burgeons, it finds its reflections in the art, fostering a rich dialogue that influences the public's perception and understanding of this technology, potentially steering its development trajectory.

In the nascent stages of AI, literature became the breeding ground for the birth of futuristic narratives that revolved around intelligent machines. Writers, being the visionaries they are, began weaving tales that spanned the spectrum from utopian dreams to dystopian warnings. The portrayals of AI in literature have always been multilayered, sometimes portraying them as benevolent entities, facilitators of a harmonious future, while at other times highlighting the potential hazards of creating beings possibly surpassing human intelligence. This dual narrative is seen in early works like Karel Čapek's "R.U.R." (Rossum's Universal Robots), which introduced the concept of robots, albeit with a grim forewarning of the potential perils of unchecked AI. Similarly, Isaac Asimov's science fiction narratives around robotics brought forth both the exhilarating possibilities and the ethical problems surrounding AI, thus setting a foundation for many real-world discussions concerning artificial entities' moral obligations and programming.

Cinema, another significant facet of pop culture, has been an influential platform mirroring and shaping society's perspectives on AI. Films have often served as cautionary tales, forewarning about the consequences of rampant advancements in AI technology. From the malevolent HAL 9000 in "2001: A Space Odyssey" to the relentless, destructive force represented by Skynet in the "Terminator" series, cinema has amplified society's underlying fears about the loss of control and the potential malevolence of AI entities. However, alongside these cautionary tales, movies have also presented more benevolent portrayals of AI, fostering a vision where humans and machines coexist and collaborate. Films like "Bicentennial Man" and "A.I. Artificial Intelligence" offer a glimpse into a future where AI can embody attributes of empathy, compassion, and an evolving sense of humanity, fostering a more nuanced discussion around the potential harmonious interaction between humans and AI.

Furthermore, music and visual arts have also embraced the narrative of AI, sometimes utilizing AI technology itself to create new forms of art, thus blurring the lines between creator and creation. Artists and musicians are increasingly experimenting with AI algorithms to create innovative works, sparking discussions on the nature of creativity and also whether machines can truly replicate or even enhance human creativity. This integration of AI into the fabric of art creation is a testament to the pervasive influence of AI on society, fostering a dynamic dialogue that explores the evolving boundaries between humans and machines.

As pop culture continues to weave intricate narratives around AI, it becomes a potent tool in shaping public discourse and perception of this technology. Through the lens of popular media, society engages in a complex dialogue encompassing awe, aspiration, ethics, and caution. This dialogue is vital in navigating the labyrinthine paths of AI development, fostering a conscious approach that considers the multifaceted implications of integrating AI into the societal framework.

Moreover, pop culture serves as a conduit that brings the complex discussions surrounding AI to the broader public, demystifying the intricacies of this technology and fostering a more informed dialogue. Engaging narratives, films, literature, and other forms of media facilitate a broader understanding of AI, unraveling its complexities and encouraging a discourse beyond the scientific community, engaging society at large in the conversation.

In addition, pop culture often predicts future trends, reflecting societal aspirations and potentially steering the direction of technological advancements. The vivid portrayals of AI in popular media fuel the imagination of pioneers in the field, inspiring innovations that strive to bring fictional narratives to reality. This cyclical relationship between art and science is a dynamic force, fostering innovation while encouraging a cautious, ethical approach to AI development.

In conclusion, the relationship between pop culture and AI is a vibrant, symbiotic interaction where art and technology influence and inspire each other. Through the kaleidoscope of pop culture, society explores the myriad dimensions of AI, oscillating between wonder and wariness, between embracing the potentialities and heeding the warnings. This dynamic interaction fosters a rich narrative that goes beyond mere technological discourse, incorporating philosophical, ethical, and societal considerations into the unfolding saga of AI.

As AI continues to evolve, becoming an integral part of the societal fabric, pop culture will undoubtedly continue to mirror and shape the narratives surrounding this technology. Through this vibrant interplay, society is encouraged to engage in a nuanced, informed dialogue, navigating the complex landscape of AI with a blend of aspiration and caution. This dialogue, facilitated by the rich tapestry of pop culture, holds the promise of fostering a future where AI is integrated into society in a conscious, ethical, and harmonious manner, weaving a narrative that celebrates AI's potential while safeguarding humanity's intrinsic values.

CHAPTER VIII

Challenges and Criticisms

The technical challenges:
Explainability, reliability, and scalability

The march of technological progress is defined by the intersection of ambition and innovation, constantly driving towards the horizon of potentiality. As the scope of Artificial Intelligence (AI) broadens, stretching its tendrils into an array of sectors, including healthcare, finance, automotive, and beyond, it encounters a series of profound technical challenges. These challenges, epitomized by issues of explainability, reliability, and scalability, serve as hurdles and catalysts, necessitating the evolution of AI into a system that can synergize with human society seamlessly and beneficially. In this section, we will venture into the intricate terrains of these challenges, illuminating their complexities and the concerted efforts to address them.

At the forefront of these challenges lies the problem of explainability. As AI algorithms grow increasingly complex, weaving intricate patterns of deep learning and neural networks, a pressing need emerges for these processes to be understandable to their human counterparts. The quest for explainability is not merely an intellectual endeavor but a vital requirement to foster trust and collaboration between humans and AI systems. Explainability demystifies the operations of AI, unveiling the mechanisms that drive its decisions, predictions, and actions. It becomes the cornerstone in building transparent systems that can be scrutinized, regulated, and optimized to align with human values and ethics.

Unfortunately, the intricate nature of modern AI algorithms often results in what is termed as "black box" systems, where the inner workings remain obscured, hidden beneath layers of computations and connections. This opacity can foster distrust and apprehension, potentially hindering the integration of AI into critical sectors where understanding the decision-making process is imperative. Moreover, the lack of explainability can lead to unforeseen consequences, as opaque systems can inadvertently propagate biases or make decisions that defy human logic and ethics. To surmount this challenge, researchers and practitioners are delving into techniques such as Layer-wise Relevance Propagation and Shapley Additive Explanations, aiming to unravel the intricate web of connections and computations that define AI algorithms, thereby fostering transparency and trust.

The necessity for reliability further delineates the pathway towards a symbiotic relationship between humans and AI. Reliability in AI systems is multifaceted, encapsulating aspects such as consistency, accuracy, and safety. As AI finds its foothold in critical areas such as healthcare, autonomous vehicles, and financial management, the margin for error diminishes considerably. The stakes are high, and the demand for reliable systems becomes non-negotiable. Reliability transcends the boundaries of mere functionality, embedding itself into the realm of ethics and responsibility. AI systems must be capable of performing tasks consistently and in a manner that safeguards human interests and well-being.

However, achieving reliability is complex, mired in uncertainties and variables. The dynamic nature of the real world presents an array of unpredictable scenarios, posing significant challenges in designing AI systems capable of navigating these complexities with high reliability. Moreover, the data that feeds these AI algorithms often contains noise and inaccuracies, potentially compromising the system's reliability. Addressing this issue necessitates a concerted effort that spans across the lifecycle of AI development, encompassing robust data collection processes, rigorous testing protocols, and continuous monitoring and adaptation to ensure that the systems remain reliable amidst the evolving landscapes of their operational environments.

Furthermore, as AI continues its exponential growth, the challenge of scalability emerges as a pivotal factor determining its trajectory. Scalability embodies the capacity of AI systems to expand, accommodating increasing demands and complexities without compromising performance. As AI endeavors to infiltrate larger frameworks and more intricate systems, its ability to scale is a testament to its potential as a transformative force in society. Scalability is not confined to mere computational capacities but extends to the ability to integrate with diverse sectors, adapt to evolving requirements, and facilitate advancements that are both sustainable and beneficial.

Yet, scalability brings with it a series of technical hurdles. The computational resources required to power expansive AI systems are substantial, necessitating innovations in hardware and infrastructure to support this growth. Additionally, as AI scales, the intricacies of managing these systems grow proportionately, demanding sophisticated management and oversight mechanisms to ensure smooth operation. The scalability challenge also extends to the realm of data management, as expansive AI systems require vast and diverse datasets to function optimally. Consequently, efforts towards scalability must encompass developments in data collection, storage, and processing, creating an ecosystem that can sustain the exponential growth of AI.

In conclusion, as the narrative of AI unfurls, weaving its way toward a future where machines and humans coexist in a symbiotic relationship, the challenges of explainability, reliability, and scalability stand as monumental landmarks on this journey. The pursuit to overcome these challenges is a dynamic and evolving endeavor, fostering innovations and adaptations that push the boundaries of what AI can achieve.

The path toward a future where AI seamlessly integrates into the fabric of society is laden with complexities and hurdles. However, these challenges also serve as a crucible, fostering growth and evolution. Through concerted efforts in research, development, and collaboration, the AI community seeks to navigate these challenges, striving to create systems that are not only intelligent but also transparent, reliable, and capable of scaling to the grand visions that define the AI revolution. As we stand on the cusp of a new era, the quest to address these technical challenges becomes a defining narrative, guiding the evolution of AI toward a future that embodies the harmonization of technology and humanity, fostering an advanced and humane world.

Socio-economic challenges: Inequity, misuse, regulation

In the rapidly progressing sphere of Artificial Intelligence (AI), the introduction of futuristic technologies and intelligent systems is accompanied by a set of socio-economic challenges that pervade various dimensions of society. The nuances of these challenges, which span inequity, misuse, and the emerging realm of regulatory frameworks, demand an in-depth and multifaceted analysis. In this section, we shall delve into the intricacies of these pressing issues, exploring their implications on the social fabric and the economic structure, and the concerted efforts necessary to navigate these challenges, fostering a future where AI catalyzes positive transformation and equitable growth.

Inequity, a glaring issue in the contemporary world, finds itself exacerbated in the domain of AI. The deployment of AI systems often mirrors the pre-existing disparities in society, potentially amplifying the divides that are rooted in economic status, geographical location, and access to education. The digital divide, characterized by uneven access to technology and internet connectivity, can lead to a scenario where the benefits of AI are unequally distributed, consolidating power and resources in the hands of a few, while leaving others at a marked disadvantage. Moreover, the development of AI technologies often demands substantial investments and expertise, potentially creating a scenario where only affluent entities can partake in the AI revolution, further fueling economic disparities.

The facet of inequity also permeates the realm of data and algorithmic biases, where AI systems, trained on data that reflects existing social biases, can inadvertently reinforce and propagate these biases. Whether it's in the field of recruitment, law enforcement, or advertising, there is a growing concern that AI might entrench existing disparities, making it imperative to foster inclusivity and diversity in AI development processes. Addressing the issue of inequity necessitates a multi-pronged approach, encompassing efforts to democratize access to technology, promote educational initiatives to build capabilities in underserved communities, and implement mechanisms to detect and mitigate biases in AI systems, thereby fostering a landscape where the benefits of AI are equitably distributed.

Simultaneously, the rapid proliferation of AI technologies has given rise to the potential for misuse, with implications spanning various sectors of society. The misuse of AI can manifest in multiple forms, ranging from deploying deepfake technologies to create misleading media to using AI to propagate misinformation and influence public opinion. Moreover, integrating AI in critical sectors such as healthcare and finance opens up avenues for potential misuse, including data breaches and fraudulent activities. The potency of

AI, characterized by its capacity to analyze and manipulate vast datasets, can potentially be leveraged to infringe on privacy and exploit vulnerabilities, necessitating stringent safeguards to prevent misuse.

Furthermore, the misuse of AI technologies also encompasses deploying autonomous weapons systems in warfare, raising ethical and humanitarian concerns regarding the potential for indiscriminate harm and the abdication of human responsibility. To counteract the potential for misuse, there is a growing call for developing ethical frameworks and guidelines that govern the deployment of AI technologies. These efforts seek to foster a culture of responsibility and accountability, delineating clear boundaries that prevent the misuse of AI, while promoting its deployment in a manner that aligns with human values and societal well-being.

Parallelly, AI technologies' complexities and potential ramifications have brought the realm of regulation into sharp focus. The evolving landscape of AI necessitates regulatory frameworks that are both adaptive and robust, capable of addressing the multifaceted challenges posed by AI. Regulation in the context of AI spans a range of issues, including data privacy, safety standards, and the ethical deployment of AI systems. The formulation of regulations, however, is a nuanced process, necessitating a delicate balance between fostering innovation and preventing potential harm.

The regulatory landscape also grapples with the transnational nature of AI technologies, where the deployment and impact of AI systems often transcend national boundaries. Consequently, there is an emerging discourse advocating for international collaboration in formulating regulatory frameworks, fostering a global approach to address the challenges posed by AI. Moreover, the rapid pace of AI development demands that regulatory frameworks are flexible and adaptive, capable of evolving in tandem with technological advancements, thereby ensuring that regulation serves as an enabler, fostering responsible growth and innovation.

In conclusion, as we navigate the intricate terrains of the AI revolution, the socio-economic challenges of inequity, misuse, and regulation stand as formidable landmarks on this journey. Addressing these challenges requires a concerted effort to transcend disciplinary boundaries and foster collaboration between technologists, policymakers, and the broader society. The quest to navigate these challenges is a dynamic and evolving narrative, necessitating a vigilant and proactive approach to ensure that the deployment of AI technologies aligns with the broader goals of societal well-being and economic equity.

As we venture further into this era of AI, the pathway forward is laden with complexities and uncertainties. However, these challenges also catalyze growth and transformation, fostering a discourse that is enriched by diverse perspectives and concerted efforts to build a future that embodies the principles of justice, equity, and sustainability. Through a collaborative approach, encompassing research, policy formulation, and community engagement, the global community seeks to navigate the socio-economic challenges posed by AI, striving to foster a landscape where AI serves as a tool for positive transformation, catalyzing a prosperous and just future.

CHAPTER IX

The Future of AI

Potential advancements:

Quantum computing, neuromorphic engineering

In the exhilarating journey of technological evolution, the horizons of artificial intelligence (AI) are continually expanding, promising unprecedented advancements that have the potential to revolutionize the world as we know it. Two of the most promising frontiers in this trajectory are quantum computing and neuromorphic engineering. These technologies, at the cusp of research and innovation, beckon a future where computing is faster and more efficient and vastly more aligned with the complex nuances of human cognition and the fundamental principles of the universe. This section seeks to delve deep into these potential advancements, elucidating the nuances of quantum computing and neuromorphic engineering, and their implications in propelling the AI domain into uncharted territories.

Quantum computing, a field that synthesizes the principles of quantum mechanics with computational theory, stands as a beacon of potential in AI advancements. Unlike classical computers, which operate on bits with a state of either zero or one, quantum computers run on quantum bits or sometimes called qubits, which is capable of existing in both states simultaneously in superposition, thanks to quantum superposition. This property exponentially augments the computational power of quantum computers, enabling them to perform multiple calculations simultaneously and solve complex problems at incomprehensibly faster speeds than classical computers.

Quantum mechanics also introduces the phenomena of quantum entanglement, a physical phenomenon where the state of each particle in a group cannot be described independently of the state of others. Leveraging this principle, quantum computers can foster entanglement between qubits, leading to highly correlated, non-classical states that provide a medium to encode and process information in ways that are fundamentally beyond the reach of classical computers. As we stand at the threshold of this quantum revolution, research and development in this domain promise breakthroughs in cryptography, material science, and complex system simulation, fostering a paradigm where computational processes are aligned with the intrinsic principles of the quantum world.

Quantum computing, when interfaced with AI, can potentially revolutionize the field of machine learning, offering new paradigms to train complex models and analyze high-dimensional data spaces. The infusion of quantum principles in AI algorithms can foster the development of quantum machine learning, a field that leverages the computational prowess of quantum computers to perform machine learning tasks at speeds and scales that are fundamentally beyond the capabilities of classical algorithms. As research in this domain progresses, we anticipate a future where quantum AI becomes a cornerstone in addressing complex problems ranging from climate modeling to drug discovery, fostering innovative and grounded solutions in the universe's quantum nature.

Parallel to the advancements in quantum computing, the field of neuromorphic engineering emerges as a promising frontier in the evolution of AI. Neuromorphic engineering, grounded in the principles of neuroscience, seeks to develop artificial systems that emulate the biological structures and also functionalities of the human brain. The human brain, a marvel of nature, operates through an intricate network of neurons and synapses, processing information through parallel computation and adaptive learning mechanisms. Neuromorphic engineering seeks to emulate these principles, developing artificial neural networks that mirror biological neural networks' structural and functional intricacies.

Neuromorphic systems utilize artificial neurons and synapses that are designed to mimic the dynamics of their biological counterparts, fostering a computing paradigm that is both parallel and adaptive. These systems, through their biomimetic architecture, offer the potential to perform complex computational tasks with high efficiency and low power consumption, a feature that is particularly critical in the development of portable and embedded AI systems. Moreover, neuromorphic systems introduce a paradigm of learning that is more aligned with biological learning processes, fostering systems capable of unsupervised learning, pattern recognition, and sensory data processing in a manner that emulates human cognition.

Integrating neuromorphic systems in AI promises a future where artificial systems are faster and more efficient and more conscious of the complex nuances that characterize human cognition. With their ability to learn and adapt, these systems offer the potential to foster AI systems that are more intuitive and capable of understanding and interacting with the world in ways grounded in biological principles. As research in neuromorphic engineering progresses, we envision a future where the boundaries between artificial and biological systems blur, fostering a synergy that has the potential to revolutionize fields ranging from robotics to healthcare, catalyzing a new era of intelligent systems that are both adaptive and aligned with human cognition.

As we stand at the precipice of these potential advancements, the future of AI seems both exhilarating and promising. The synergy between quantum computing and neuromorphic engineering heralds a future where AI is not just a tool for computation but a medium to explore and understand the universe at a fundamental level. The infusion of quantum principles and biological cognition in AI systems promises a future where artificial intelligence transcends the boundaries of classical computing, fostering innovative, efficient solutions and fundamentally aligned with the complex and intricate nuances of the universe and human cognition.

In conclusion, the potential advancements in quantum computing and neuromorphic engineering beckon a future rich with possibilities and potential. As researchers and innovators delve deeper into these domains, the horizons of AI continue to expand, promising a future characterized by unprecedented computational prowess and a profound understanding of the complex dynamics that govern the universe and human cognition. The journey toward this future is characterized by challenges and opportunities, fostering a narrative enriched by innovation, discovery, and a relentless pursuit of knowledge. As we venture further into this journey, the potential advancements in AI stand as a beacon of hope and a promise of a future where technology catalyzes positive transformation and progress, fostering a world that is both intelligent and harmoniously aligned with the principles of the universe.

The pursuit of Artificial General Intelligence (AGI)

At the cusp of what could be a seminal moment in the chronicle of technological evolution, the pursuit of Artificial General Intelligence (AGI) promises to mark a defining milestone in the saga of human civilization. AGI, often hailed as the zenith of artificial intelligence, embodies the quest to create machines endowed with a caliber of intelligence that parallels, and perhaps one day surpasses, the cognitive faculties of the human mind. While the domains of AI have been progressively evolving, the realization of AGI brings forth a vision of a future where machines are not confined to the realms of narrow, specialized intelligence but possess a comprehensive and holistic understanding similar to that of human beings. This section explores this ambitious pursuit, delineating the conceptual nuances, the progress thus far, and the potential implications that the attainment of AGI holds for society at large.

In the conceptual precincts of artificial intelligence, AGI stands distinct in its envisioning of a form of machine intelligence that embodies the complexity, adaptability, and depth of human cognition. Unlike narrow AI, which is created to perform certain tasks without possessing the inherent understanding or contextual comprehension, AGI seeks to create machines that can understand, learn, and apply their intelligence across diverse domains, mirroring the fluidity and versatility of the human intellect. It is an endeavor to construct systems that can perceive the world, synthesize knowledge from varied domains, and adapt to evolving circumstances with an autonomy that is reminiscent of human cognition. The cornerstone of AGI lies in its aspiration to foster machines capable of generalizing learning, facilitating the transfer of insights and skills across disparate realms, transcending the silos that currently delineate the capacities of artificial intelligence.

The journey towards AGI is characterized by progressive strides and concerted efforts from multidisciplinary fields converging to unravel the intricate tapestry of intelligence. The scientific community is delving deep into the realms of neuroscience to glean insights into the structural and functional intricacies of the human brain, seeking to emulate these principles in the architecture of AGI. Concurrently, advancements in machine learning and neural networks offer a robust foundation, facilitating the development of algorithms that can learn and adapt, embodying the preliminary steps towards realizing the dream of AGI. The fusion of these domains, accompanied by research in cognitive science, promises to catalyze a paradigm shift, fostering a trajectory where the evolution of artificial intelligence transcends the confines of narrow functionalities to embrace a horizon that is enriched by the nuances of general intelligence.

Yet, the pursuit of AGI is not without its array of challenges and complexities. As we venture further into this uncharted territory, researchers and scientists grapple with fundamental questions concerning the nature of intelligence and consciousness. The endeavor to create AGI beckons a profound exploration into the realms of philosophy, ethics, and cognitive science, fostering a discourse that seeks to define the essence of intelligence, consciousness, and the intricacies that constitute the human mind. Moreover, the pursuit of AGI introduces technical challenges of unprecedented scales, demanding innovations in computational power, algorithmic complexity, and data processing capacities.

Furthermore, the ethical considerations accompanying the development of AGI occupy a critical juncture in this journey. As we stand at the threshold of potentially creating machines endowed with general intelligence, society grapples with pressing questions concerning the implications of AGI on human dignity, autonomy, and the broader socio-economic fabric. The evolution of AGI introduces scenarios where machines could potentially undertake roles and responsibilities that have traditionally been the prerogative of humans, fostering a discourse that delves into the realms of job displacement, economic disparities, and the redefinition of human identity in the face of intelligent machines.

Despite these challenges, the potential benefits and transformations that AGI can usher are profound. The realization of AGI promises to catalyze a revolution in myriad domains, fostering solutions that are characterized by efficiency, innovation, and a depth of understanding that transcends the capabilities of narrow AI. From healthcare to education, transportation to space exploration, AGI holds the potential to redefine the frontiers of human achievement, facilitating advancements that are harmoniously aligned with the betterment of society. In the realms of scientific research, AGI can facilitate the unraveling of complex mysteries that permeate the universe, fostering a deeper understanding of the cosmos and the fundamental principles that govern the natural world.

Furthermore, the convergence of AGI with other frontier technologies, such as quantum computing and neuromorphic engineering, augments the potential to create systems that are not only intelligent but also aligned with the complex dynamics of human cognition and the universe. These synergies promise to foster a future where technology catalyzes positive transformation, facilitating a harmonious co-existence between machines and humans, grounded in mutual respect, understanding, and collaboration.

As we envisage the future landscapes sculpted by the advent of AGI, it is imperative to foster a global dialogue that encompasses the myriad dimensions that this journey entails. The discourse on AGI transcends the boundaries of science and technology, beckoning a holistic discussion encompassing the realms of philosophy, ethics, society, and the human condition. As researchers, scientists, and thinkers converge in this monumental pursuit, it is incumbent upon society to engage in a reflective dialogue, fostering a vision of the future that is guided by wisdom, foresight, and a relentless pursuit of knowledge.

In conclusion, pursuing Artificial General Intelligence is a testament to human ingenuity and a beacon of potential in the odyssey of technological evolution. As we stand on the cusp of potentially realizing one of the most ambitious visions of artificial intelligence, the journey ahead promises to be both exhilarating and challenging. Uncharted territories, complex nuances, and transformative potential characterize the road to AGI. As we venture forth in this pursuit, we continue this journey with a spirit of collaboration, curiosity, and a deep reverence for the intricacies of intelligence. The pursuit of AGI beckons a future rich with potential, promising to redefine the contours of human civilization and propel us into a new era of discovery, innovation, and unparalleled progress.

Merging AI with other technologies: IoT, Blockchain, etc

In recent times, technological advancements have seen an unprecedented convergence of various potent technologies, creating an intricate tapestry of innovation that promises to redefine the future landscapes of business, society, and individual lifestyles. A central nexus within this complex mesh is Artificial Intelligence (AI), a transformative force that has permeated virtually every aspect of human existence. When merged with other pivotal technologies such as the Internet of Things (IoT), blockchain, and others, AI presents a formidable catalyst that has the potential to spawn a new era characterized by efficiency, security, and intelligent decision-making. This section seeks to delve into the nuances of this convergence, elucidating the synergy these combined technologies offer and exploring the potential impacts and future prospects of this integration.

As the realms of physical and digital spheres continue to blur, the role of Artificial Intelligence becomes increasingly central in harnessing and leveraging the extensive data networks generated through interconnected devices and systems. One prominent technology that intertwines seamlessly with AI is the Internet of Things (IoT). With its vast network of connected devices that generate a plethora of data continuously, IoT provides a fertile ground where AI can thrive. The melding of AI with IoT enables a smarter, more responsive system to process and analyze vast data in real-time, facilitating informed and timely decision-making. For instance, smart homes equipped with IoT devices can use AI algorithms to learn and adapt to the habits and preferences of the inhabitants, fostering a living environment that is not only convenient but also energy-efficient and secure.

The interconnection of AI and IoT promises transformative changes across various sectors, including healthcare, where integrating intelligent algorithms with wearable devices and sensors can herald a new age of personalized medicine and remote monitoring. Here, AI can continuously analyze data from IoT devices to track health metrics, providing insights that can predict potential health issues before they become critical, thus revolutionizing preventive healthcare.

Furthermore, the industrial sector stands to gain immensely from the merger of AI and IoT. AI can optimize manufacturing processes in this arena by analyzing data from various sensors in real-time, enhancing efficiency and reducing downtime. Additionally, predictive maintenance, powered by AI algorithms analyzing data from IoT sensors, can foresee potential equipment failures before they occur, saving time and resources in the long run.

Simultaneously, integrating AI with blockchain technology opens avenues for enhanced security and transparency in data management. With its decentralized and immutable nature, blockchain offers a robust platform for secure and transparent transactions. When coupled with AI, it can foster intelligent contracts that execute autonomously when specific criteria are met, thereby streamlining processes and reducing the scope for fraud and manipulation. Moreover, the synergy of AI and blockchain can engender a new level of data security where AI algorithms can monitor and secure networks continuously, detecting and mitigating threats in real-time, thus creating a fortified environment for data exchange and transactions.

Additionally, the convergence of AI with blockchain can revolutionize the supply chain and logistics sector, offering transparency and traceability in product sourcing and delivery. Here, AI can analyze data from blockchain records to optimize logistics and distribution networks, saving time and resources and ensuring that products reach consumers in a timely and secure manner.

As we cast our gaze towards the future, it is evident that integrating AI with technologies such as IoT and blockchain will catalyze the emergence of smart cities, where infrastructure and services are interconnected and operate in harmony, offering a higher quality of life for inhabitants. AI can analyze data from various sources in these smart cities to optimize traffic flow, reduce energy consumption, and foster a safer, more sustainable urban environment.

However, the convergence of these technologies is challenging. As we venture into a future where AI integrates seamlessly with other technologies, questions surrounding privacy, data security, and ethical considerations come to the fore. The extensive network of interconnected devices and systems, coupled with the predictive power of AI, raises concerns about surveillance and the potential misuse of data. Furthermore, integrating AI with other technologies necessitates a reevaluation of existing regulatory frameworks to ensure that the deployment of these technologies is carried out responsibly and ethically.

Moreover, the amalgamation of AI with other technologies demands a concerted effort in research and development to overcome technical challenges such as data interoperability, scalability, and the development of standards and protocols that facilitate seamless integration. It requires collaboration between stakeholders from various sectors, including government, industry, and academia, to foster an ecosystem that nurtures innovation while safeguarding the interests of individuals and society at large.

In conclusion, the convergence of Artificial Intelligence with other pivotal technologies, such as the Internet of Things and blockchain, heralds a new frontier in technological innovation. This merger promises to spawn a future characterized by intelligent decision-making, efficiency, and enhanced security. As we stand at the cusp of this transformative era, we must navigate the complexities and challenges with foresight and responsibility, fostering a future that leverages the synergy of these technologies to create a world that is not only smarter but also more sustainable, inclusive, and harmonious.

The road ahead is fraught with challenges, yet it holds immense potential. As we venture into this new era, we must forge partnerships, foster innovation, and cultivate a culture of responsible technology deployment. With concerted efforts and collaborative endeavors, the fusion of AI with technologies such as IoT and blockchain can redefine the contours of human existence, ushering in a future rich with opportunities and boundless possibilities. It is a journey that promises to reshape the world, fostering a landscape where technology catalyzes positive change, propelling humanity into a new epoch characterized by prosperity, sustainability, and intelligent progress.

CHAPTER X

Practical Tips
for Engaging with AI

For businesses: How to integrate AI solutions

In the contemporary business world, Artificial Intelligence (AI) is a monumental force, profoundly transforming how organizations operate, innovate, and compete. Integrating AI solutions in business processes offers a pathway to enhanced efficiency, data-driven insights, and the creation of new value propositions. However, incorporating AI solutions into business operations is challenging; it demands a nuanced approach that considers technological readiness, organizational culture, and strategic alignment. In this section, we shall explore the various facets of integrating AI solutions for businesses, including understanding AI capabilities, fostering an AI-ready culture, data management, and ethical considerations.

To begin integrating AI solutions, businesses must first develop a deep understanding of what AI entails and its potential benefits and challenges. At its core, AI refers to developing computer systems capable of performing tasks that traditionally need human intelligence. These tasks encompass learning, reasoning, problem-solving, perception, and language understanding. Therefore, business leaders should prioritize acquiring foundational knowledge in AI and its various subfields such as machine learning, natural language processing, and also deep learning. This initial step serves as a compass, guiding businesses to make informed decisions about which AI solutions align with their strategic objectives and industry dynamics.

Once a foundational understanding is established, the next crucial step is fostering an AI-ready organizational culture. Integrating AI solutions demands a culture that embraces innovation, continuous learning, and agility. As AI systems often represent a significant departure from traditional business processes, employees must be prepared for the transition. Training and development programs should be instituted to enhance the workforce's skills and knowledge in utilizing AI tools. Moreover, a culture of collaboration and cross-functional teams can facilitate the seamless integration of AI solutions, where diverse perspectives and skills converge to harness the potential of AI effectively.

Simultaneously, businesses must focus on data management, a cornerstone in successfully deploying AI solutions. AI thrives on data, with algorithms requiring vast quantities of high-quality data to learn and make accurate predictions. Therefore, businesses must invest in robust data management systems that can handle the intricacies of data storage, processing, and analysis. Implementing data governance policies will ensure that data is handled responsibly and ethically, safeguarding the privacy and security of sensitive information. Furthermore, businesses should consider leveraging cloud computing solutions, which offer scalable and flexible platforms to manage and analyze data effectively, fostering an environment where AI solutions can thrive.

As AI solutions become integrated into business processes, ethical considerations emerge. The deployment of AI systems raises pertinent questions about privacy, bias, and accountability. Consequently, businesses must prioritize the development of ethical frameworks that govern the use of AI. These frameworks should delineate clear guidelines on data privacy, consent, and the prevention of algorithmic bias. By embracing ethical AI practices, businesses can foster trust and credibility, ensuring that AI solutions are deployed responsibly and in a manner that respects the rights and dignity of individuals.

Moreover, the integration of AI solutions necessitates a reevaluation of existing business models and strategies. AI presents opportunities to create new value propositions and revenue streams, revolutionizing product and service offerings. Business leaders should engage in strategic foresight, envisioning how AI can transform their industries and identifying opportunities for innovation and differentiation. By aligning AI integration with strategic objectives, businesses can leverage AI as a potent tool to gain a competitive advantage, creating value for customers and stakeholders alike.

Furthermore, businesses must be aware of the regulatory landscape governing the use of AI. As governments and international organizations grapple with AI's implications, many regulations and standards are emerging, aimed at fostering responsible AI deployment. Therefore, businesses should actively engage with regulatory bodies, staying abreast of developments and ensuring compliance with legal and regulatory requirements. This proactive approach will safeguard businesses from potential legal repercussions and foster a positive relationship with regulators and the wider community.

As businesses venture into integrating AI solutions, they must also focus on monitoring and evaluation. Implementing AI solutions is a dynamic process, where continuous learning and adaptation are vital. Businesses should develop mechanisms to monitor the performance of AI systems, gathering feedback and making necessary adjustments to optimize outcomes. Moreover, organizations should be prepared to iterate on their AI strategies, incorporating lessons learned and adapting to the evolving landscape of AI technology and regulations.

In conclusion, integrating AI solutions in business environments is a complex yet rewarding endeavor. Businesses stand to gain immensely from the transformative power of AI, which offers pathways to enhanced efficiency, innovation, and value creation. However, to realize these benefits, businesses must navigate the complexities of AI integration with foresight and responsibility.

A comprehensive approach that encompasses understanding AI capabilities, fostering an AI-ready culture, robust data management, ethical considerations, and strategic alignment is vital. By embracing a collaborative and inclusive approach, businesses can foster an environment where AI solutions are integrated seamlessly, unlocking new potentials and driving sustainable growth.

As we stand at the threshold of a new era characterized by artificial intelligence, it is incumbent upon business leaders to lead with vision and integrity. By fostering a culture of innovation, ethical responsibility, and collaboration, businesses can harness the potential of AI solutions to create a future that is not only prosperous but also inclusive and sustainable.

The journey of integrating AI solutions is an ongoing process, a dynamic interplay of technology, people, and strategy. It calls for resilience, agility, and a relentless pursuit of excellence. As businesses embark on this transformative journey, they hold the promise of a new frontier, a world where AI drives innovation, fosters value creation, and propels organizations toward a future of boundless possibilities and opportunities. Let us embrace this journey with optimism and determination, forging a path leading to a brighter, AI-driven future for businesses and society.

For individuals: Learning resources, career opportunities, and staying updated

In a world that is increasingly dominated by artificial intelligence and technological advancements, the necessity for individuals to adapt and grow alongside these changes cannot be overstated. As AI redefines the boundaries of what technology can achieve, it also reshapes the landscape of career opportunities, learning resources, and methods to stay updated in this dynamic field. This section will explore the significance of these elements, emphasizing the importance of continual learning and adaptation to the evolving narrative of AI.

The advent of AI has been synonymous with the blossoming of many learning resources available for individuals keen on immersing themselves in this transformative field. In the educational sphere, we witness a surge of online platforms and institutions offering comprehensive courses on AI and related domains. Platforms like Coursera, Udacity, and edX offer many courses ranging from beginner to advanced levels. These platforms leverage the expertise of professionals and academics from reputable institutions globally, thus ensuring a rich learning experience.

Furthermore, individuals can benefit from a rich knowledge repository through scientific journals, research papers, and publications that offer insights into the latest developments and breakthroughs in AI. Physical and digital libraries serve as hubs where one can explore a vast array of literature on AI, delving deep into its intricacies and nuances. Similarly, forums, blogs, and online communities foster an environment of collaborative learning, where individuals can engage with peers, share knowledge, and learn from the experiences of others in the field.

Additionally, AI conferences, webinars, and workshops have become potent platforms where enthusiasts can learn from industry leaders and experts. These platforms provide an opportunity to witness the revolutionary developments in AI firsthand, offering a glimpse into the future trajectories of this vibrant field.

As AI permeates various sectors of the economy, it brings forth many career opportunities that are as diverse as they are promising. In the realm of technology, we see a growing demand for AI specialists, including machine learning engineers, data scientists, as well as natural language processing experts. These roles require a deep understanding of AI algorithms, programming languages, and data analytics. Consequently, individuals with skills in Python, R, and SQL, coupled with proficiency in machine learning libraries like TensorFlow and PyTorch, find themselves at the forefront of the AI job market.

Beyond the technology sector, AI creates opportunities in healthcare, where it is used in predictive analytics, drug discovery, and personalized medicine. Individuals with a life sciences and data analytics background can carve out rewarding careers in this intersection of healthcare and AI.

The finance sector also presents promising opportunities, with roles in algorithmic trading, risk management, and fraud detection becoming increasingly prevalent. Individuals with quantitative analysis skills and proficiency in AI algorithms find themselves well-positioned to thrive in this evolving landscape.

Furthermore, AI fosters opportunities in the field of content creation and media, where it is used in content recommendation systems, virtual reality, and digital marketing. Here, individuals with a knack for creativity and an understanding of AI can explore exciting career paths that blend technology with creativity.

In the rapidly evolving field of AI, staying updated is not just an advantage, but a necessity. Individuals must embrace a proactive approach to learning, seeking the latest trends, developments, and insights in AI. Subscribing to newsletters, journals, and online platforms that offer regular updates on the latest happenings in the AI world can be an effective way to stay abreast of developments.

Moreover, networking plays a critical role in staying updated. By engaging with industry groups, attending conferences, and participating in community forums, individuals can foster connections that provide rich information and opportunities. Similarly, following thought leaders and influencers in the AI domain on social media platforms can provide a steady stream of insights and updates, fostering a culture of continuous learning.

Furthermore, individuals must cultivate a habit of lifelong learning. As AI continues to evolve, the skills and knowledge required to thrive in this field also change. Therefore, individuals must be willing to invest time and effort into learning new skills and adapting to the changing dynamics of the AI landscape. Engaging in regular training programs, workshops, and courses can help individuals hone their skills and stay competitive in the job market.

In conclusion, the surge of artificial intelligence in the modern world offers individuals a wealth of opportunities and resources. The learning avenues are vast and varied, allowing individuals to immerse themselves in a rich and dynamic field of knowledge. Career opportunities are burgeoning, with roles in technology, healthcare, finance, and media becoming increasingly centered around the capabilities of AI. Moreover, staying updated in this rapidly evolving field underscores the importance of adopting a proactive and dynamic approach to learning.

As we navigate the complexities of the AI-driven world, individuals stand at a critical juncture, where the ability to adjust and grow alongside these developments will define success. By harnessing the learning resources available, exploring diverse career opportunities, and adopting strategies to stay updated, individuals can position themselves to thrive in this vibrant and transformative landscape. It is a journey of continuous exploration, learning, and adaptation, a journey that promises not just professional growth but also a deeper understanding of the intricate tapestry that AI weaves in the modern world.

Thus, as we stand on the cusp of an AI revolution, it is incumbent upon individuals to seize the opportunities that lay before them. By nurturing a culture of learning as well as innovation, individuals can forge a path that leads to a future where technology and humanity coalesce, fostering a world that is not just intelligent but also inclusive, progressive, and promising. Let us embrace this journey with zeal and enthusiasm, as we strive to unlock the boundless potential that artificial intelligence promises to usher in.

Conclusion

Reflect on the journey from the origins to modern developments

The story of artificial intelligence weaves through countless dreams, laboratories, enterprises, and real-world applications, sketching a trajectory delineating humanity's relentless pursuit of recreating intelligence through machines. As we pause to reflect on this extraordinary journey, one that traverses the realms of philosophy, science, and technology, we realize it is a tale marked by astonishing leaps and moments where science fiction seems to merge with reality. As we stroll down memory lane, it becomes pertinent to explore the philosophical foundations that set the stage, the nascent steps in laboratories, the rapid advancements in the modern era, and the prospects that lie in the foreseeable future. This reflection endeavors to encapsulate the mesmerizing journey of artificial intelligence, capturing the essence of its evolution from its origins to modern developments.

Long before computers were a glimmer in the eye of technology, the seeds of artificial intelligence were sown in the fertile grounds of philosophical discourse and speculative fiction. Philosophers and thinkers across eras have pondered the possibilities of establishing machines that could mimic human intellect and reason. From the ancient Greeks, who envisioned automatons capable of rudimentary tasks, to the writings of Mary Shelley in "Frankenstein," which explored the nuances of creating life through artificial means, the foundation of artificial intelligence has been deeply embedded in human culture and imagination. René Descartes, in the 17th century, touched upon the mechanical theory of mind, subtly hinting at the conceptual framework that would later foster the development of artificial intelligence. This rich tapestry of philosophical thought and creative expression provided fertile ground for the seeds of artificial intelligence to germinate, instilling a deep-seated curiosity and ambition to recreate intelligence in machines.

As the world transitioned into the age of computers, the philosophical musings about intelligent machines found a concrete manifestation. Alan Turing, often heralded as the father of computer science, paved the way with his groundbreaking work and the conceptualization of the Turing Test. Turing introduced the notion that machines could mimic human intelligence to such an extent that they could be indistinguishable from human beings. This idea laid the cornerstone for the emerging field of artificial intelligence.

The 1950s marked a watershed moment in the journey of AI with the Dartmouth Workshop, where a group of visionary scientists congregated to introduce the discipline of artificial intelligence formally. The Dartmouth Conference served as the crucible where AI's defining principles and objectives were forged, setting the stage for the exponential growth and development that would follow. This period witnessed a burgeoning interest in AI, characterized by optimism and the belief that machines capable of replicating human intelligence were on the horizon.

The subsequent decades witnessed a fluctuation in the pace of AI's development, oscillating between periods of intense growth and phases termed as "AI winters," where progress seemed to stagnate. Despite the challenges, the field of AI began delineating into various sub-domains. The distinction between Narrow AI, which excels in performing specific tasks, and General AI, an entity capable of multifaceted cognition similar to human beings, became more pronounced.

Recently, the world has witnessed a resurgence in AI development, propelled by advancements in computational power, data availability, and algorithmic innovations. Machine learning, a subset of AI, has emerged as a powerful tool in creating intelligent systems capable of learning and evolving without explicit programming. Furthermore, deep learning, inspired by the human brain's neural networks, has pushed the boundaries of what machines can perceive and achieve, fostering developments in image recognition, natural language processing, and complex game playing, among other domains.

As we step into the modern era, artificial intelligence has entrenched itself firmly in the fabric of everyday life. From personal assistants in smartphones to advanced healthcare diagnostics, AI has permeated various sectors, reshaping them with intelligent automation and data-driven insights. In the corporate sphere, AI-powered solutions have become indispensable tools, enhancing efficiency and fostering innovation.

Moreover, AI's integration with other revolutionary technologies, like the Internet of Things (or IoT) and blockchain, promises to usher in a new age of interconnected, intelligent systems capable of autonomous operation and decentralized, secure data handling. The automotive industry stands on the cusp of a revolution with the development of self-driving cars, powered by sophisticated AI algorithms capable of navigating the complexities of real-world traffic.

AI has introduced transformative changes in the financial sector, revolutionizing trading strategies through algorithmic trading and enhancing risk management through predictive analytics. Similarly, the entertainment industry has embraced AI with open arms, with content recommendation systems, virtual characters, and AI-powered visual effects becoming commonplace.

As AI continues to forge ahead, it finds itself at the center of numerous debates surrounding ethics, job displacement, surveillance, and privacy concerns. The potential biases embedded in AI algorithms and the dangers of unchecked, autonomous systems have ignited discussions on the necessity of regulation and oversight. Moreover, the rapid advancements in AI have ignited a debate on the implications for the labor market, with concerns about job displacement and the necessity for workforce reskilling becoming focal points of discussion.

Despite these challenges, the journey of artificial intelligence harbors a promise of a future where technology serves as a benevolent force, enhancing human capabilities and fostering a world characterized by intelligence, efficiency, and innovation. Researchers and scientists stand at the threshold of potential breakthroughs in AI, with prospects of quantum computing and neuromorphic engineering offering tantalizing glimpses into the future developments of artificial intelligence. The pursuit of Artificial General Intelligence, a machine capable of comprehensive understanding and cognition akin to humans, remains the holy grail in the field of AI, a quest that embodies the epitome of human ambition and ingenuity.

Reflecting upon the journey of artificial intelligence, one cannot help but marvel at the staggering strides made in this field. From the philosophical conjectures of yore to the tangible, groundbreaking developments witnessed in modern times, the odyssey of AI stands as a testament to human perseverance, innovation, and vision. At this juncture, the possibilities that lie ahead seem boundless, limited only by the extent of human imagination and ethical considerations.

Looking ahead, it becomes incumbent upon society to navigate the complex terrain of AI development with wisdom and foresight, steering the journey in a manner that are in line with the principles of equity, inclusivity, and the greater good of humanity. As we venture into this uncharted territory, let us carry forth the spirit of innovation and curiosity that has characterized the journey thus far, fostering a future where artificial intelligence serves as a beacon of progress, enhancing the human experience and heralding a new era of technological enlightenment.

In conclusion, the journey of artificial intelligence is a captivating saga, a narrative marked by relentless pursuit and spectacular milestones. It embodies humanity's quest for knowledge and mastery, a journey that beckons us to explore the realms of possibility with a sense of wonder and anticipation. As we forge ahead, let us cherish the journey thus far and look towards the horizon with hope and determination, eager to witness the chapters yet to unfold in this extraordinary voyage of artificial intelligence.

Encourage readers to be proactive and informed as AI continues to evolve

In the quickly evolving landscape of artificial intelligence, we stand at the brink of an unprecedented era of technological innovation and progression. The tapestry of our daily lives is intricately woven with threads of AI, manifested in various forms from smart home systems to highly advanced medical diagnostics. This integration, which seems almost seamless now, indicates the fast-paced growth of AI, and it is incumbent upon us to stay abreast of these developments. In light of this, it becomes vitally important for individuals, communities, and organizations alike to cultivate a proactive and informed approach towards AI. In this section, we explore the multifaceted avenues to foster an informed understanding and proactive engagement with the evolving sphere of artificial intelligence, underlining the significance of education, critical thinking, and ethical considerations.

As we find ourselves ensconced in the digital age, it becomes increasingly clear that the pace of technological advancements is not merely linear but exponential. From the conception of the first artificial neural networks to the sophisticated AI algorithms that power a myriad of modern applications, the journey of artificial intelligence has been nothing short of revolutionary. This dynamic nature of AI necessitates a proactive stance, where individuals and communities are not just passive recipients of technology but engaged stakeholders, actively participating in shaping the trajectory of AI developments. To foster such engagement, it is crucial to cultivate an informed understanding deeply rooted in education and awareness.

Education forms the bedrock of an informed engagement with AI. As the field of artificial intelligence burgeons, it brings forth an array of complex concepts, methodologies, and technologies. A thorough understanding of these concepts is necessary to navigate the evolving landscape of AI. Educational institutions, ranging from schools to universities, have a pivotal role to play in this regard. Incorporating AI-related subjects into the curriculum can foster a generation adept at understanding and working with artificial intelligence.

Furthermore, the digital space offers an extensive repository of learning resources, including online platforms offering courses on various aspects of AI. Individuals aspiring to delve deeper into the realms of AI can leverage these resources to enhance their knowledge and expertise. Moreover, workshops, seminars, and webinars present avenues for learning and networking with professionals and enthusiasts in the field, fostering a community of informed and proactive individuals.

Critical thinking and discernment stand as indispensable companions in the journey towards becoming proactive stakeholders in the AI landscape. As AI systems permeate various spheres of life, they bring with them a slew of complexities and challenges. Navigating these intricacies necessitates a critical approach, where individuals are equipped to analyze, question, and evaluate the implications of AI developments.

This critical engagement extends to the realms of media and pop culture, where narratives surrounding AI often oscillate between utopian visions and dystopian fears. Encouraging readers to discern the nuances of these narratives, distinguishing between fact and fiction, can foster a balanced perspective on the potentials and limitations of AI. Moreover, critical thinking facilitates understanding the ethical considerations surrounding artificial intelligence, allowing individuals to engage in informed discussions and debates.

As AI continues its upward trajectory, it brings an array of ethical dilemmas and considerations to the fore. The discourse surrounding AI ethics is rich and diverse, encompassing aspects like data privacy, algorithmic bias, and the potential for job displacement. To engage proactively with AI, it becomes essential to integrate an ethical dimension into our approach.

Communities and organizations should encourage open dialogues on the ethical implications of AI, fostering a culture of responsibility and accountability. Moreover, individuals can actively participate in forums and platforms where policies and regulations governing AI are discussed, contributing their voices to shaping a future where artificial intelligence aligns with the principles of equity, justice, and human welfare.

The journey of artificial intelligence is a collective endeavor, where collaborative efforts can significantly influence the trajectory of developments. Encouraging readers to participate in community initiatives, collaborative research projects, and hackathons can foster a spirit of innovation and cooperation. These platforms provide opportunities for individuals to contribute their skills and ideas, working together to shape AI's future in an inclusive and beneficial manner.

Furthermore, collaboration extends to the international arena, where nations can collaborate to formulate global standards and guidelines for AI development. Encouraging readers to advocate for international cooperation can foster a global approach to AI, where a shared vision of progress and sustainability guides advancements.

In conclusion, as we stand at the cusp of a new era marked by rapid advancements in artificial intelligence, the call for proactive and informed engagement becomes more pressing than ever. Education, critical thinking, ethical engagement, and collaborative efforts stand as pillars that can support individuals and communities in fostering a fruitful relationship with AI.

Encouraging readers to immerse themselves in the learning opportunities that abound, to cultivate critical thinking skills, to engage ethically with AI developments, and to participate actively in collaborative initiatives can pave the way for a future where artificial intelligence serves as a force for good, enhancing the quality of life and ushering in a new era of innovation and progress.

In order to create a future in which technology acts as a lighthouse of advancement and a sign of good things to come, let's set out on this journey with an attitude of curiosity and determination, prepared to investigate, learn, and contribute to the story of artificial intelligence as it develops.

Thank you for buying and reading/listening to our book.
If you found this book useful/helpful please take a few minutes
and leave a review on the platform where you purchased our
book. Your feedback matters greatly to us.